The Struggle for Development

For Mjriam

The Struggle for Development

Benjamin Selwyn

polity

First published in 2017 by Polity Press

Polity Press
65 Bridge Street
Cambridge CB2 1UR, UK

Polity Press
350 Main Street
Malden, MA 02148, USA

ISBN-13: 978-1-5095-1278-2
ISBN-13: 978-1-5095-1279-9 (pb)

A catalogue record for this book is available from the British Library.

Library of Congress Cataloging-in-Publication Data

Names: Selwyn, Ben, author.
Title: The struggle for development / Ben Selwyn.
Description: Cambridge, UK ; Malden, MA : Polity Press, 2017. | Includes
    bibliographical references and index.
Identifiers: LCCN 2017004330 (print) | LCCN 2017020101 (ebook) | ISBN
    9781509512812 (Mobi) | ISBN 9781509512829 (Epub) | ISBN 9781509512782
    (hardback) | ISBN 9781509512799 (pbk.)
Subjects: LCSH: Economic development.
Classification: LCC HD82 (ebook) | LCC HD82 .S428 2017 (print) | DDC
    338.9--dc23
LC record available at https://lccn.loc.gov/2017004330

Typeset in 10 on 16.5pt Utopia Std by Servis Filmsetting Ltd, Stockport, Cheshire
Printed and bound in Great Britain By Clays Ltd, St Ives PLC

For further information on Polity, visit our website:
politybooks.com

Contents

Preface and Acknowledgements

This book contributes to development thinking, policy and practice in two ways. The vast majority of development literature and policy analyses are based upon elitist conceptions of social change, where states and corporations are identified as primary development actors. This book, by contrast, views social change from the bottom up. Its first contribution is to conceptualise development from the perspective of labouring classes. Doing so provides an answer to the puzzle of expanding (and highly concentrated) wealth in a sea of global poverty. Secondly, it contends that collective actions by labouring classes, far from undermining development, which is how elite conceptions of social change portray them, generate real human development. Once this two-part argument is grasped, then the project of seeking to engender human development assumes a new perspective.

Some of the chapters in this book draw upon and develop arguments previously published. Part of chapter 3 was published as a Centre for Global Political Economy working paper (no. 10, 2016). Parts of chapters 4 and 5 were published in *Third World Quarterly* (both vol. 7, 2016).

In writing this book I have incurred many intellectual debts. First and foremost, my colleagues in the Historical Materialism World Development Research Seminar (HMWDRS) continue to provide the most stimulating forum within which to collectively understand and apply Marxist political economy to contemporary capitalism. Over the years HMWDRS has included Liam Campling, Satoshi Miyamura, Jon Pattenden, Gavin Capps, Elena Baglioni, Owen Miller, Alessandra Mezzadri, Sam Ashman, Helena Pérez Niño, Demet Dinler, Jeff Webber, Penny Howard and Kristian Lasslett.

Many people have read parts of this book and/or discussed it with me and in the process have suggested improvements. They include Tom Selwyn, Andy Sumner, Thomas Pogge, David Woodward, Luke Martell, Adam Fishwick, Felipe Antunes, Lucia Pradella, Ray Kiely, Mary Mellor, Siobhán McGrath, John Minns, Leslie Sklair, Peter Newell, Tom Marois, David Ockwell, Julian Germann, Sam Knafo, Earl Gammon, Andreas Bieler, Kalpana Wilson, Feyzi Ismail, Haroon Akram-Lodhi, Carlos Oya, Tony Norfield, Paul Cammack and Juanita Elias.

I am truly lucky to work alongside wonderful colleagues in the Department of International Relations and in the Centre for Global Political Economy (CGPE) at the University of Sussex. Rorden Wilkinson and Andrea Cornwall, as head of department and head of school respectively, deserve special thanks as they have worked extra hard to generate creative time and space for colleagues to pursue their research. Students at Sussex, at undergraduate, MA and PhD level, are simply marvellous and have, over the years, provided much critical stimulation to my thinking about global development.

I am deeply indebted to four brilliant thinkers who, knowingly or not, helped me construct my intellectual foundations. These are Henry Bernstein, Chris Harman, Ellen Meiksins Wood and Michael Lebowitz.

I am very grateful to John Minns, director of the Australian National Centre for Latin American Studies (ANCLAS) at the Australian National University, who made it possible for me to spend six fantastic weeks conducting research and writing at the centre in late 2015.

I thank Louise Knight, Nekane Tanaka Galdos, Clare Ansell, Caroline Richmond and David Held at Polity for supporting this project.

Our daughter Valentina has provided continuous entertainment over the last three years. Most profoundly, I thank my wife Mjriam, who supported me all the way through this and previous labours, and who has always pushed me to explain my ideas with more clarity. To her I dedicate this book.

'The great are only great because we are on our knees. Let us rise up.'

Louis-Marie Prudhomme, *Révolutions de Paris*

1

The Big Lie

Introduction

In his dystopic novel *1984*, George Orwell depicts a world of perpetual war, total government surveillance and infinite ideological manipulation of the population. The novel's main character, Winston, describes how the state pursues ideological manipulation through the practice of doublethink, which he defines as follows:

> To know and not to know, to be conscious of complete truthfulness while telling carefully constructed lies, . . . to use logic against logic, to repudiate morality while laying claim to it . . .. To tell deliberate lies while genuinely believing in them, . . . to deny the existence of objective reality and all the while to take account of the reality which one denies. (Orwell 1977: ch. 3, ch. 9)

In this book I argue that contemporary reasoning about development, as propounded by institutions such as the United Nations, the International Labour Organization, the World Bank, many non-governmental organisations, state leaders and the mass media, represents a giant exercise in doublethink. It is based on an endlessly repeated set of interlinked claims:

1 that continued economic growth represents the surest route towards poverty reduction and development;

2 that a rising number of people across the world are enjoying the fruits of this development;

3 that this improvement is due to their increasing participation in global markets; and

4 that it is possible to envision a world free of poverty within our lifetimes.

These arguments, and those actors and institutions that promote them, are here labelled the Anti-Poverty Consensus (APC).[1]

Global capitalism and human impoverishment

Global capitalism is an immense wealth-generating system. Despite the chronic global economic crisis that emerged in 2007, total global wealth (the sum total of money and other assets) continues to multiply. In 2013 it reached an all-time high of US$241 trillion, an increase of 68 per cent since 2003. The Swiss-based financial organisation Credit Suisse estimates that total global wealth will reach US$345 trillion by mid-2020.[2] While some of this wealth is a product of new financial technologies and instruments, and might thus be labelled fictitious, its growth represents a general trend within capitalism – of systemic wealth accumulation. This growing pot of wealth is generated by the continual transformation of nature into products (and the services and information required to sell and use them) performed by an ever-expanding global labouring class.

If economic growth and expanding global wealth are the determinants of an improving world, then the APC is correct. But total wealth itself tells us nothing about either the conditions of the world's population or the health of the planet. Capitalism's core social relations – the exploitation of labour by capital and endless competition between firms – ensure that, rather than eliminating them, economic growth reproduces inequality, poverty and environmental destruction.

Ending global poverty through economic growth alone will take more than 200 years (based on the World Bank's inhumanly low poverty line of $1.90 a day) and up to 500 years (at a more generous poverty line of $10 a day) (Hoy and Sumner 2016; and see chapter 2). The damage to the natural environment caused by several more hundreds of years of capitalist growth would wipe out any gains in poverty reduction (see Woodward 2015).

APC proponents seldom enquire into the conditions under which such wealth is produced and distributed. When they do, such enquiries are guided by the presumption that employment benefits workers. In this way, the APC seeks to disable any genuine investigation into ways in which capitalism, and in particular the capital–labour relation, is, itself, the cause of global poverty.

But let us consider the following data:

- in 2015, sixty-two individuals owned the same wealth as 3.6 billion people, the bottom half of humanity;
- the wealth of the richest sixty-two people increased by 44 per cent between 2010 and 2015 – an increase of over half a trillion dollars – to US$1.76 trillion;
- during the same period, the wealth of the bottom 50 per cent of humanity fell by over US$1 trillion – a drop of 38 per cent. (Hardoon et al. 2016)

Global wealth continues to concentrate. By early 2017 the richest eight men in the world owned the same wealth as the bottom half of humanity (Oxfam 2017). Speaking as a member of the US's capitalist class, billionaire Warren Buffett has commented that 'there's been class warfare going on for the last 20 years, and my class has won.'[3] The data above show that this class warfare, from above, is a global phenomenon.

If the world was governed by just principles, these data would generate a genuine, open and public consideration of whether wealth concentration is predicated upon the proliferation of poverty. But it is not. Orwellian doublethink cloaks capitalism's exploitative social relations and their destructive effects in emancipatory clothing. The APC proclaims loudly and ceaselessly that globalisation is good for the poor. Based on an international poverty line of $1.90-a-day purchasing power parity, the World Bank claims that, in 2015, the proportion of the world's population living in extreme poverty fell to under 10 per cent.[4] (The concept of purchasing power parity will be explained in chapter 2.)

This figure and the interpretations derived from it are weak, to say the least. It derives from the generation and application of an inhumanly low poverty line to calculate global poverty levels. The claim that global poverty is low and falling is entirely dependent upon where the poverty line is set. Slightly higher poverty lines (which are still, in reality, very low) show persistently high (and, depending on the poverty line, sometimes increasing) levels of global poverty over the last four decades.

Sanjay Reddy and Thomas Pogge (2010: 42–54) show, for example, that, when global poverty is measured according to the World Bank's 'official' poverty line (which used to be $1.25 a day), it decreased by 27 per cent between 1981 and 2005. However, if a slightly higher poverty line of $2.00 a day is used, during this period poverty increased by 1 per cent. A poverty line of $2.50 a day reveals an increase of 13 per cent. Such considerations extend beyond academic discussion. For example, using the World Bank's poverty line, the poverty rate in Mexico in the early 2000s was approximately 5 per cent. However, according to Mexican federal government poverty measures, approximately 50 per cent of the national population suffered from poverty (Boltvinik and Damián 2016: 176–7).

World Bank claims that global poverty is low and falling do not tally with data on global hunger trends. The Food and Agriculture Organization (FAO) generates data about daily calorie intake based on 'normal' (white-collar-type) activities and 'intense' activities (such as working in fields, plantations, factories and mines). In 2012, based upon calorie requirements to support normal activities, 1.5 billion people were hungry. For people undertaking intense activities, the numbers suffering from hunger increased from around 2.25 billion in the early 1990s to approximately 2.5 billion in 2012 (FAO 2012; Hickel 2016: 759–60). Many experts on poverty argue that the World Bank's poverty line is much too low, and they recommend that it be raised significantly, so that it is between four and ten times higher (Edward 2006; Woodward 2010; Pritchett 2006; Sumner 2016; and chapter 2 below). At these levels, the majority of the world's population lives in poverty.

The anti-poverty consensus

The anti-poverty consensus (APC) consists of numerous institutions across the political spectrum, ranging from the United Nations, the World Bank, the International Monetary Fund and the World Trade Organization to, perhaps more surprisingly, the International Labour Organization and many 'progressive' institutions, organisations and intellectuals. *The Economist* expresses succinctly the core of APC ideology: 'Most of the credit [for global poverty reduction] . . . must go to capitalism and free trade, for they enable economies to grow – and it was growth, principally, that has eased destitution.'[5] To be sure, some APC institutions such as the World Bank (and *The Economist*) are more liberal, while others such as the International Labour Organization are more 'interventionist'. The former argues that states must support market expansion, while the latter argues for closer state involvement and intervention in markets to protect and promote labour standards. Both, however, maintain that poor country integration into global capitalist markets (under the correct conditions) and continued economic growth represent the surest path to poverty reduction.

The anti-poverty consensus portrays capitalist development in win–win terms, where the correct type of global integration benefits capital and labour. But this win–win scenario is a myth. It is a lie sold to the world's poor in order to legitimate continued capital accumulation and economic growth. In reality, the APC justifies and contributes to global wealth concentration while hiding the continual impoverishment of the world's majority. It rationalises the oppression and exploitation of the world's poor in the name of helping them. It presents as solutions to poverty the causes of poverty. Its arguments are supported by sophisticated pseudo-scientific methods. The APC's win–win portrayal of capitalist development contributes to the delegitimation and physical repression of forms of human development that do not correspond to its model of perpetual economic growth.

However, the APC's core claim – that continuous economic growth represents the surest way to achieve generalised human development – is being rejected increasingly across the globe. For example, Pope Francis, speaking to (perhaps on behalf of) a broad constituency of the world's poor, argues that capitalism imposes 'the mentality of profit at any price, with no concern for social exclusion or the destruction of nature.' Further, 'this system is by now intolerable: farm workers find it intolerable, labourers find it intolerable, communities find it intolerable, peoples find it intolerable. The earth itself . . . finds it intolerable.'[6]

The anti-poverty counter-consensus

It is not only this book that argues against the APC. There is powerful, vocal, and often popular opposition to the APC which highlights many of its limitations and suggests alternative, state-led or state-assisted, development strategies. It is advanced by writers such as Amartya Sen, Joseph Stiglitz, Thomas Piketty, Branco Milanović, Mariana Mazzucato, Ha-Joon Chang, Robert Wade, K. S. Jomo, Dani Rodrik, Erik Reinert and many other critics of neoliberal global capitalism. This opposition is labelled here the anti-poverty counter-consensus (APCC).

This counter-consensus punches big holes in the APC's narrative. It demonstrates the mendacity of the World Bank's $1-a-day poverty line and how it manipulates evidence to generate favourable results (Wade 2004; Milanović 2011). It illustrates the inequality-inducing effects of neoliberalism (Piketty 2014). It shows the erroneous basis of neoliberal growth theory and the deleterious impacts of neoliberal policies for developing countries (Stiglitz 2007; Rodrik 2003; Jomo 2001). It explains, historically and theoretically, how economic growth, structural diversification and technological upgrading require an active state role (Mazzucato 2013; H.-J. Chang 2002; Wade 1990; Reinert 2007). Some of these authors promote a benign vision of human-centred development (Sen 1999).

Despite these critiques, however, the APCC shares much common ground with the APC. In fact more unites the two than divides them. Both hold that sustained economic growth represents the foundation upon which human development can be achieved. For example, Jomo argues that 'the only sustainable basis for mass poverty reduction involves economic growth, development policy and employment creation' (2016: 36). Similarly, in their popular book *Reclaiming Development*, Ha-Joon Chang and Ilene Grabel aim to promote 'rapid economic growth that is equitable, stable and sustainable' (2004: i).

The APC and APCC share the following common assumptions:

- economic growth is the basis for human development;
- growth is based upon capital–labour relations where capital is free to manage the labour process independently of workers' influence;
- capitalist property rights are necessary, and the right of the capitalist investor to their profit is sacrosanct;
- poverty is caused by malfunctioning capitalist markets, not by capitalism per se;
- the capital–labour relation cannot be the source of oppression and/or exploitation as it is freely entered into by workers and capitalists.

Authors in the APCC argue for, and passionately believe in, the possibilities of achieving a benign global capitalism. In all of these ways the APC and the APCC generate an image of capitalism as a sphere of (potential) developmental opportunity. Neither school considers how capitalism is a system that operates through exploitation, oppression and unpaid-for wealth appropriation. Nor do they examine the systematic evacuation of democracy from the economic sphere. Without addressing these questions, however, it is impossible to understand properly the great paradox of global capitalism – systematic wealth generation in the midst of widespread poverty.

Global poverty, inequality and wealth concentration are intrinsic to capitalism. These phenomena reflect not lack of resources, wealth or mal-integration into capitalist markets but capitalism's particular exploitative social relations, wedded to an institutional denial of democracy across large swathes of social life. As the late Ellen Meiksins Wood wrote, the essence of the capitalist economy is that

> a very wide range of human activities, which in other times and places were subject to the state or to communal regulation of various kinds, have been transferred to the economic domain. In that ever-expanding domain, human beings are governed not only by the hierarchies of the workplace but also by the compulsions of the market, the relentless requirements of profit-maximization and constant capital accumulation, none of which are subject to democratic freedom or accountability. (Wood 2012: 317; see also Cammack 2002; Harman 2002b; Bernstein 2010; Lebowitz 2010)

Capitalism's economic sphere, where workers are directly exploited by capital, must remain devoid of democracy. If democracy were to penetrate and flourish within the workplace, and workers could make choices about resource allocation and working conditions, the disciplinary power of capital would begin to crumble.

Is it possible to think of and generate forms of human development that are not rooted in capitalist social relations? This book argues that such an objective is possible and, moreover, that myriad attempts to establish alternative forms of human development are occurring at present across the globe. To comprehend such attempts better, however, it is necessary to approach development from the perspective of labouring classes.

From labour-centred to labour-led development

A labour-centred approach requires viewing development from the perspective of labouring classes. The concept of labour-centred development (LCD) is deliberately broad, and it encompasses a variety of strategies designed to ameliorate labouring-class conditions. These range from what may be called enlightened elite policies to activities undertaken by labouring classes themselves. This book's labour-centred development approach can be divided into three sub-processes. These are:

- *pro-labour development*: where state actors design policies and enact policies that benefit workers;[7]
- *labour-driven development*: where workers' collective actions push states and capital to make concessions to labour;
- *labour-led development*: where workers' collective actions aim to generate, and succeed in generating, tangible gains for them and their communities.

An example of *pro-labour* development feeding into *labour-driven* development is the recent Mahatma Ghandi Rural Employment Guarantee Act in India. This act pledges 100 days' paid employment to every rural household as a state-led strategy for overcoming rural destitution (Carswell and De Neve 2014). The Act, as Jon Pattenden (2016) shows, has in turn given confidence to rural labourers to bargain for better conditions (labour-driven development) and to begin to combat the widespread existence of servitude in the Indian countryside.

The establishment of the European and North American welfare states represents a high point of labour-driven development. Following

the 1917 Russian Revolution, class struggles in both regions intensified. The human development gains of the European working classes
after the Second World War were due not to the generosity of capitalists
and states but to the threat of mass unrest from below: 'If you don't give
the people social reform, they will give you social revolution', Quintin
Hogg, a leading light in the Tory Party, told the British Parliament in
1943 (cited in Cliff and Gluckstein 1996: 211).

Often, the lines between different sub-processes of LCD are blurred.
More progressive development thinkers sometimes conceive of radical
development policies as entailing a pro-labour dimension. We certainly welcome more, rather than less, pro-labour and labour-driven
development policy.

The core argument of this book, however, is that labouring-class
movements and struggles against capitalist exploitation can be, and
are, developmental in and of themselves. Labouring classes can do
more than wait for pro-labour policy or try and influence it. *Labour-led
development refers to processes where labouring-class collective actions
directly generate meaningful improvements to their and their communities' livelihoods.*

Democratically organised collective actions by labouring classes
can engender prefigurative forms of human development where they
bring about democratic ends – in terms of political, economic and cultural institutions, participation, and decision-making over resource
generation and use (Boggs 1977: 100). Such actions herald ways of
bringing about human development that are qualitatively more democratic, participatory and emancipatory than the visions of development
proposed by the APC or the APCC. These deep democratic impulses
emerge, repeatedly, through labouring-class collective actions as they
challenge capitalism's authoritarian social relations.

Class analysis

This book adopts Marx's class-relational approach to explain the apparent paradox of rising global wealth and continued poverty. Class, here, is understood as a *relationship of exploitation* where capitalist classes extract surplus value from labouring classes. Under capitalism, workers are systematically paid less than the value they produce for their employers (Marx [1867] 1990; and see chapter 2).[8]

Since Marx began his work, the claim that capitalism has been fundamentally transformed has been advanced, alongside arguments for abandoning his emancipatory political economy. For example, in their popular (and opaque) *Empire*, Michael Hardt and Antonio Negri (2000: 293) argue that the new 'post-industrial'/information economy is generating and reliant upon 'immaterial' forms of labour, which consequently render previous Marxist class analysis redundant. Such labour consists of 'analytical and symbolic tasks' (intellectual or linguistic work, such as computer programming, public relations, media work and graphic design) and 'affective labour' (including carers, fast-food workers and legal assistants).

The argument that capitalism is dynamic, that it changes, and that, therefore, so too do the form and content of the working class is a truism to any serious Marxist. However, the claim made by writers such as Hardt and Negri, that contemporary capitalism is 'post-industrial', and that Marx's analysis of it is therefore out of date, often assumes that capitalism was 'industrial' in his day. As Terry Eagleton (2011: 169) notes, however: 'In Marx's own time, the largest group of wage labourers was not the industrial working class but domestic servants, most of whom were female. The working class, then, is not always male, brawny and handy with a sledgehammer.' Further, the concept of 'immaterial' labour is bogus. All human labour combines immaterial/intangible (thought) activities and material/tangible (physical) activities.

While this book's conception of class is derived from Marx, it rejects much of what passes for, and is presented as, Marxist class analysis. G. A. Cohen presents a pretty mainstream Marxist version of class analysis when he writes that 'A person's class is established by *nothing but his objective place* in the *network of ownership relations*. His consciousness, culture, and politics do not enter the *definition* of his class position' (Cohen 1978: 73, emphasis added). Anthony Giddens (2009: 1113) also presents Marxist class theory in these terms. This definition correctly highlights the social organisation of the means of production as a determinant of class location, where capitalists own them and workers need to sell their labour power to access them to earn a wage. However, it obscures how class *relations* are lived experiences. It represents an attempt to generate a purely objective and structural (but ultimately lifeless) conception of class. In doing so, however, it downplays the importance of subjective elements of class. To transcend this limitation, I draw upon recent innovative approaches to social reproduction theory (cf. Luxton and Bezanson 2006; Ferguson 2008; Weeks 2011; Ferguson and McNally 2015; see below).

Three limiting consequences follow from adopting a purely structuralist conception of class. First, in its generation of a dichotomy between 'objective' class structure/location and lived 'experience', it contributes to a simple approach to class politics. It is often assumed by structural Marxists that workers are predisposed to a particular (class-based, progressive and even revolutionary) political orientation. As E. P. Thompson argued, however, such a conception of class generates misleading political expectations: "'It", the working class, is assumed to have a real existence, which can be defined almost mathematically. Once this is assumed it becomes possible to deduce the class-consciousness which "it" ought to have (but seldom does have)' (Thompson 1963: 9).

A second consequence of such structuralist conceptions is that they privilege 'class' over 'other' forms of oppression, such as gender/sexuality and race/ethnicity. The political implications of such positions are paradoxical, to say the least. Marxists that privilege 'class' over other forms of social oppression effectively underwrite the political marginalisation (and heightened exploitation) of oppressed groups that cannot be classified in rigid 'class' terms. Such marginalisation in turn further fragments labouring classes and facilitates capital's greater exploitation of them.

Third, the above definition of class, as a position in the network of ownership relations, de-emphasises collective political action as a determinant of class relations. By contrast, Marx and Engels observed that 'The separate [labouring class] individuals form a class only insofar as they have to carry on a common battle against another class; otherwise they are on hostile terms with each other as competitors' (Marx and Engels [1932] 1970: 82). Class, therefore, is something 'which in fact happens (and can be shown to have happened) in human relationships' (Thompson 1963: 8). It is not, then, only an 'objective place in the network of ownership relations'.

One-sided structural conceptions of class risk deadening the sensual (real) social dynamics through which classes are formed, relate, and regard themselves and each other. Paradoxically, such conceptions obscure the genuine expressions and experiences of the class relations which Marxists/socialists hope are the basis for their emancipatory socialist project.

The *social relational* conception of class adopted here seeks to overcome the dichotomies and privileging associated with structural conceptions – in particular the dichotomy of 'class' over 'non-class' forms of oppression. Class relations of exploitation (re)produce themselves via myriad forms of hierarchical and oppressive social relations, such as gender, race and sexuality, and vice versa (McNally 2015). They are, as Himani Bannerji writes, 'social relations and forms [that] come into being in and through each other' (Bannerji 1995: 149; see also Mohanty 2003). For these reasons, it is proper to expect labouring class formations, movements and, thus, processes of labour-led development to be highly diverse.

The global labouring class: an introduction

The global labouring class is the foundation upon which global wealth is generated and concentrated. The term labouring or working classes refers here to 'the growing numbers . . . who now depend – directly *and indirectly* – on the sale of their labour power for their own daily reproduction' (Panitch et al. 2001: ix, emphasis added). The International Labour Organization estimates that the global labour force numbered over 3 billion by the mid-2000s (Kapsos 2007). The global labouring class is expanding rapidly, is diverse, and is highly fragmented.

The global labouring class includes unpaid women workers largely responsible for social reproduction in the household, urban/industrial employed workers ('the working class' in traditional Marxian terminology), urban and rural unemployed workers, 'informal' workers that populate the ever-expanding urban slum lands, many members of the peasantry, and many members of the so-called emerging developing-world middle class (see chapter 2). While the global labouring class takes myriad forms, it shares a common condition – its subordination to and exploitation by capital. In this way it constitutes a 'unity of the diverse' (Marx [1939] 1993: 101).

It is erroneous conceptually to reduce the labouring class to employed formal-sector workers, which is what some Marxists do and what many critics of Marxism say it does. As Harry Cleaver noted, referring to an earlier phase of global collective actions:

> The identification of the leading role of the unwaged in the struggles of the 1960s in Italy, and the extension of the concept to the peasantry, provided a theoretical framework within which the struggles of American and European students and housewives, the unemployed, ethnic and racial minorities, and Third World peasants could all be grasped as moments of an international cycle of working-class struggle. (Cleaver 2000: 73)

Six mega-trends, of class decomposition and recomposition, intertwining with new and old hierarchies and forms of oppression, underpin the expansion and fragmentation of the contemporary global labouring class. First, mass dispossessions (de-peasantisation) have swept the global South. Peasantries and rural labour forces have been pushed off the land following its commercialisation for agri-business, its appropriation for non-agricultural use, and as a consequence of the increasing difficulties of sustaining small-scale agricultural production. Most starkly, for example, in China some 270 million people left the countryside for the towns between 1980 and the present, by far the largest migration in global history (Ren et al. 2016: ix; see also Walker and Buck 2007).

Second, there has been a huge expansion of the (increasingly female) industrial working class across the global South.[9] The ILO calculates that the percentage of the world's industrial labour force located in 'less developed regions' expanded from 34 per cent in 1950, to 53 per cent in 1980 (ILO 2008), and to 79 per cent in 2010 (Smith

2016: 103). In a similar vein, the International Monetary Fund suggests that the number of labourers working in export-orientated industries quadrupled between 1980 and 2003 (IMF 2007: 162).

A third mega-trend has been the expansion of the numbers of the global unemployed. Already by the late 1990s, 'one billion workers representing one-third of the world's labour force, most of them in the South, were either unemployed or underemployed' (Davis 2006: 199). Under the direction of multinational firms, the global information technology revolution, which could contribute to genuine human development, is exacerbating mass unemployment. As Cornell University Professor Kaushik Basu (2016) notes:

> Digital innovations over the last three decades now enable people to work for employers and firms in different countries, without having to migrate. . . . As the march of technology continues, these strains will eventually spread to the entire world, exacerbating global inequality – already intolerably high – as workers' earnings diminish.

Fourth, insecure employment is on the rise across the globe. India represents perhaps the front runner in the casualisation race, where over 90 per cent of work is informal (Prashad 2016). In the United States, labour economists Lawrence Katz and Alan Krueger (2016: 1) report that 'The percentage of workers engaged in alternative work arrangements – defined as temporary help agency workers, on-call workers, contract workers, and independent contractors or freelancers – rose from 10.1 percent in . . . 2005 to 15.8 percent in . . . 2015.'

Fifth, the expansion of the world's labouring class is not simply a function of push and pull factors (for example, land grabs and urban work opportunities). It is based upon increased women's labour inside and outside the household, which is often organised along global lines. As Amy Hite and Jocelyn Viterna observe:

> In households facing enormous financial pressures, women responded by employing a series of strategies within the household, by organizing their communities to demand government assistance, and by going to work or increasing the amount of time that they spent on paid labor . . . Women's roles as 'shock absorbers' only increased their vulnerability in the work place, as vanishing household resources necessitated their increased acquiescence to poor working conditions. (2005: 54)

In addition to their unpaid domestic labour, by the mid-2000s around 67 million women worked as paid domestic labourers for other families, including more than 11 million migrant care workers[10] (see also Yeates 2004; Elias and Gunawardana 2013).

Global capitalism reproduces itself through an increasingly large, fragmented and exploited labouring class, from which it exacts a terrible human developmental price. The sixth mega-trend, however, represents the potential source for a transformation of these conditions. Even before the onset of the current global economic crisis, the US geo-strategist Zbigniew Brzezinski described a situation where 'In the twenty-first century the population of much of the developing world is . . . politically stirring. It is a population conscious of social injustice to an unprecedented degree and resentful of its deprivations and lack of personal dignity' (Brzezinski 2007: 203).

Accumulating resentment among labouring classes represents a social tinderbox, where sparks can detonate mass collective unrest. These revolts can be toxic as well as potentially emancipatory. As an example of the former, in April 2016 a wave of violence spread across parts of South Africa, directed at immigrants from Zimbabwe, Malawi and Mozambique.[11]

However, the energy of labouring-class collective actions, when channelled against capital and its political-institutional supports, can represent a transformative and genuinely developmental social dynamo. At the time this book was completed, large-scale collective actions reverberated across much of the global South. Throughout 2015, 2016 and into 2017 in South Africa, mass student struggles for free education intensified. In September 2016, between 150 and 180 million Indian workers waged a general strike against continued anti-labour state policies. Starting in June 2016 in Argentina, large-scale demonstrations and strikes by women workers sought to highlight and combat gender inequality and violence against women. A mass strike on 19 October demanded 'higher and equal salaries, an end to precarious and informal labour, longer parental leaves that include fathers, workplace nurseries, and effective prosecution in cases of workplace abuse, violence, and discrimination' (Zorzoli 2016). During November and December 2016, South Korean workers protested against their corrupt president, Park Guen-hye, and for her impeachment. A protest in December involving more than 2 million pushed the National Assembly to begin impeachment procedures.

Perhaps most remarkably, decades-long mass struggles by Chinese workers have won them significant wage increases. Between 2005 and 2006, average hourly wages in China's manufacturing sector trebled.[12]

Whether or not such movements begin to realise their latent potential to generate novel developmental dynamics depends upon their successful collective mobilisation. That potential, however, is vital to comprehending genuinely emancipatory development.

The rationale and organisation of this book

In contrast to the APC and the APCC, this book aims to explain and define human development from the perspective of the world's labouring classes. While many critical and left-field accounts of contemporary development bemoan the effects of neoliberalism and globalisation upon the world's labouring classes, they then argue for more benign state, corporate and NGO actions to help the latter. In doing so, they legitimate elite-dominated social change. This book argues, conversely, that those exploited by global capitalism are also those that can and do transform the meaning, objectives and processes of human development.

The book is organised as follows. Chapter 2 critiques the anti-poverty consensus's '$1-a-day' conception of poverty. It shows why and how it minimises the extent of global poverty and how it is now being used to promote the idea of a rising global middle class. It then outlines theoretically why and how capitalist exploitation, appropriation and oppression are the core causes of global poverty.

Chapter 3 analyses the dynamics of contemporary global capitalism. According to APC institutions such as the World Bank and the International Labour Organization, poor-country integration into global value chains (GVCs) represents the surest path to economic growth and poverty reduction. The chapter shows how, on the contrary, the proliferation of GVCs is predicated upon the expansion of a super-exploited and impoverished global labouring class. It therefore renames GVCs global poverty chains.

Chapter 4 discusses how a wide range of development theories – neoliberal, statist and some Marxist – conceive of capitalism as a progressive sphere of developmental opportunity and justify the oppression and exploitation of labouring classes. It argues that these theories are based upon a fundamental contradiction – the advocacy of labour exploitation and oppression in the name of ameliorating labour's condition.

Chapter 5 moves beyond critique towards solutions by introducing the theory of labour-led development (LLD), providing empirical examples and arguing that it represents a really existing strategy and process of human development.

Chapter 6 completes this book by providing a vision of what a labour-led development process could look like. It is not a blueprint. Rather, it is advanced in a spirit of democratic participation – a spirit that must be the essence of labour-led development. The intention of this book is to reconceptualise human development as a process of resisting and overcoming capitalist exploitation and to stimulate thinking and actions that contribute to that objective.

Capitalism and Poverty

Introduction

The core argument of the anti-poverty consensus is that global poverty has been falling since the 1980s and is now at historically low proportions. Its decline has been generated by poor countries' increased participation in global markets. On this basis, the APC argues for yet more global integration.

In what follows, section 2.2 shows how the APC's poverty calculations are designed to understate vastly the incidence of global poverty. It also critiques APC claims that, as a consequence of the reduction in poverty, contemporary capitalism is generating a fast-growing global middle class. Section 2.3 provides an alternative, class-relational approach to investigating capitalism's polarising and poverty-inducing tendencies.

Global poverty analysis as doublethink

In rich capitalist countries, absolute poverty is understood in relation to the rest of the country's population. For example, in the UK, absolute poverty is defined in terms of an income-derived minimum *acceptable* standard of living.[1] An acceptable standard of living is, by definition, socially defined. In order to determine poverty trends, such a poverty line is reasonably easy to understand and to apply.

This is not the way that the World Bank calculates global poverty. The Bank and the APC promote an asocial (non-relational), absolute understanding of poverty based upon very low poverty lines. This section outlines the way in which poverty is calculated by the Bank and its ideological role in bolstering the anti-poverty consensus. It shows what is wrong with its methodology and suggests the beginnings of an alternative mode of poverty analysis.

According to the World Bank, the number of people living on less than its notional figure of $1 a day fell from 1.943 billion in 1990 to 0.894 billion in 2012 (iresearch.worldbank.org/povcalNet/). It claims, further, that in 2015 the percentage of the world's population living in extreme poverty fell to under 10 per cent.[2] For these reasons, the World Bank group president, Jim Yong Kim, argues that 'This is the best story in the world today – these projections show us that we are the first generation in human history that can end extreme poverty.'[3]

The foundation stone of the World Bank's analysis, findings and subsequent policy orientation is the measurement and calculation of extreme poverty. In its 1990 *World Development Report* (World Bank 1990), it established international poverty lines (IPLs), which are commonly defined as $1 a day ('extreme poverty') and $2 a day ('poverty') for household members. The $1-a-day poverty line was originally conceived after Martin Ravallion, the director of the World Bank's research department, found that the poverty lines of eight poor countries (a number of which were initially set by the Bank) were very close to this amount (Ravallion et al. 1991; Pogge 2010: 66). Ravallion has admitted that these choices were 'frugal' and 'deliberately conservative' (cited in Woodward 2010).

These frugal poverty lines, devised by World Bank researchers, do not reflect assessments *by* the poor about their daily survival requirements. Nor are they concerned with inequality as a determinant of poverty. In this way they (perhaps purposely) direct analysis towards the collection of data about the poor rather than trying to understand how the poor exist and reproduce themselves through relations with the non-poor.

The IPL for extreme poverty has been increased, the Bank argues, to reflect changes in relative price levels across countries, to $1.08 in 1993, to $1.25 in 2005, and to $1.90 in 2015.[4] Notably, however, the upper threshold of $2 a day has not been updated consistently with the lower threshold IPL.[5] Despite these increases in the IPL base line, it is still popularly referred to in $1-a-day terms. In order to keep things as clear as possible, I will adopt this practice here.

The base line and the base year of the IPL are expressed in PPP terms – for example, $1.25 (2005 PPP) or $1.90 (2015 PPP). PPP stands for purchasing power parity. In principle, PPP dollars denote the cost in a local currency of purchasing the same amount of goods as could have been purchased in the US in a given year. As Thomas Pogge (2010: 68) puts it, 'the Bank counts someone who, in India or Vietnam, is living on the exchange-rate equivalent of $0.40 or $0.45 per day in 2005 as being non-poor because this amount, converted at 2005 PPPs, equals or exceeds $1.25.'

The Bank's poverty analysis is founded upon four logical steps (see Reddy and Pogge 2002; Reddy 2006: 170).

1 Determine a base line and base year. (As noted above, the base lines and base years have evolved – from $1.00 in 1985, to $1.08 in 1993, to $1.25 in 2005, and to $1.90 in 2015.)
2 Apply the IPL *spatially*: convert the amount at base-year PPPs into local currency units.

3 Apply the IPL *temporally*: use national price data to determine the costs of consuming the same goods in different years.

4 Calculate, using household surveys, the numbers of the population able to consume daily above or below the value of '$1 a day' in the various country/year locations.

If a person attains a daily consumption of the value of $1 or above, they are counted as not poor. If it is under $1, they are counted as poor. The value of their consumption is established by using price data from the relevant country and year to calculate the market prices of what they consume. This means that, if a person consumes a range of goods without having to pay for them, perhaps because they have their own plot of land to grow food, the value of these goods can be calculated to establish the value of their daily consumption.

The Bank's primary concern in establishing the IPL was to calculate the incidence of and trends in global poverty. The establishment of the $1-a-day poverty line was hardwired into international policy, discourse and ideology through the UN's formulation of the Millennium Development Goals (MDGs) and subsequent Sustainable Development Goals (SDGs). In what follows, it will be argued that the way the World Bank has employed its conception and measurement of poverty demonstrates its attempt to generate a methodology and results that shield it from criticism and portray positively its pro-globalisation agenda. This is so in at least six ways.

First, the $1-a-day conception of poverty is 'money-metric' in that it defines the international poverty line 'in relation to a money amount rather than an explicit conception of human well-being' (Reddy 2006: 170). *Such a conception does not actually tell us if a person could stay alive at this consumption level.* Moreover, it hides other multidimensional causes of poverty by reducing poverty alleviation to a particular monetary-value level of consumption. Such an approach excludes considerations such as the numbers of hours and types of work required to earn above the poverty threshold (Reddy 2006: Cimadamore et al. 2016: 7). If a worker is able to consume more than the equivalent of $1 a day but engages in life-threateningly long, arduous, risky or hazardous labour to do so (for example, scavenging), then she or he is counted as non-poor by the Bank. Further, if people consume the equivalent of the value of the poverty line by getting into debt, by using savings, by selling assets or by stealing, they would be counted as 'non-poor'. The Bank's methodology also ignores the cost of health and education, which are free in some countries and very expensive in others.

Second, the World Bank claims that its generation of a money-metric IPL was designed to generate an 'objective' measure of the level of consumption required by the poor to avoid extreme poverty. It did this by using national poverty lines (often fixed by the Bank itself) to 'look . . . at the prices of the foods that make up the diets of the poor' (World Bank 1990: 27). This methodology is beset by a circular (and cruel) reasoning. The food consumed by those living at the poverty line is considered sufficient for their survival rather than as a product of their poverty (and thus extremely limited choices). A poverty line grounded in a reasonable conception of human needs should be based on the calculation of a healthy diet (which is more easily attained by the non-poor) rather than on the (often poor-quality) diets of the poor. If a healthy diet of a non-poor (perhaps middle-class) person was considered as essential to avoid poverty, then the $1 base line would have to be higher. This would in turn require a higher IPL and would reveal that a larger percentage of the world's population live under the poverty line than is claimed by the Bank.

Third, the Bank's initial use of the lowest poverty lines to construct its IPL artificially inflated the purchasing power of the world's poor.

Had the IPL been generated by combining the poverty lines of higher-income countries and converting them into dollars, then the base line would have been higher (Edward 2006). For example, in 2011 the Bank calculated that, in India, 300 million people lived below the IPL and also claimed that the incidence of poverty in the country was declining. However, in the same year approximately 900 million people in India were living on fewer than 2,100 calories a day. Further, the proportion of the population consuming insufficient calories has increased – from 58 per cent in 1984, to 64 per cent in 2005, to around 75 per cent in 2011 (Prashad 2014).

Fourth, the PPP-based IPL is designed to exclude 'subjective' aspects of poverty and thereby restricts the conception of poverty to consumption. The rationale behind this decision is that 'subjective' aspects of poverty are prone to immeasurable variation across regions and time and therefore preclude Bank-style poverty analysis. For example, it argues that 'in some countries piped water inside a dwelling is a luxury, but in others it is a "necessity"' (World Bank 1990: 27). But, as Boltvinik and Damián (2016: 177) put it, the Bank 'assumes food to be the sole human need, leaving all other needs fully unmet . . . thus adopting a conception that reduces human beings to the status of animals.'

The Bank's distinction between 'objective' and 'subjective' aspects of poverty is bogus. Its adoption of a $1-a-day money-metric poverty line and its demarcation of 'subjective' and 'objective' aspects of poverty represent its own subjective decisions. It could have decided to formulate a more generous and socially encompassing poverty line. While this would also have been a subjective decision, it would have been a more realistic one. Had it done so, the Bank's methodology would have generated a very disturbing image of a world where, rather than the image required to support its optimistic, pro-globalisation narrative, deep-seated poverty predominates. Depending on where they are set, higher poverty lines would reveal less steep poverty reduction or even an increase (chapter 1; Pogge 2010: 64).

Fifth, as the former World Bank researcher Lant Pritchett (2006) argues, the $1-a-day (extreme poverty) and $2-a-day (poverty) IPLs make little sense because anyone living just above the $2 threshold is still poor. Indeed, the World Bank's adoption of these poverty lines generates an image of the rich countries of the world virtually free from (either extreme or 'normal') poverty.

Sixth, the Bank's methodology of using household surveys to calculate consumption levels is gender-blind. It does not account for intra-household gender (or generational) inequalities. Rather, it assumes that household members consume equally, and consequently it disregards differing poverty burdens of women and men (Kabeer 2003: 81).

The $1-a-day IPL represents an ideology-driven exercise in doublethink. This is apparent when it is applied to Northern country populations. The '$1-a-day line is . . . equivalent to living on about £0.60 per person per day in the UK in 2007. This means a family of four living on an income of about £75 a month' (Woodward 2010: 12). In the mid-2000s, the IPL was 'equivalent, after allowing for inflation, to living in the USA with just $1.3 dollars to spend each day to meet all your survival needs' (Edward 2006: 382). In India in 2007, the $1-a-day equivalent was 9 rupees, or under 25 cents.[6]

The $1-a-day poverty line has institutionalised a double standard in global politics. On the one hand an (inhumanly low) absolute poverty measurement is deemed appropriate for counting the poor in poor countries and informing their 'development' policy. On the other hand, governments in rich countries use relative poverty measurements to calculate national poverty levels and to formulate social policy. This double standard can be interpreted as one of the latest versions of orientalist (racist) othering (Said 1979).

The wealth produced daily and accumulated historically within the global system means that very rapid poverty alleviation (at a much more generous poverty line than propounded by the APC) is feasible (Sumner 2016; and see chapter 6). That such a redistribution of wealth is kept off the political agenda by the APC reveals the low importance it attaches to genuine poverty alleviation.

Alternatives to the $1-a-day international poverty line

Numerous attempts have been made to devise more humane poverty lines and to calculate trends of world poverty. Peter Edward (2006) argues that an 'ethical' poverty line would reflect people's abilities to achieve a normal life expectancy (of about 74 years). Such an IPL would be between 2.7 and 3.9 times higher than the Bank's IPL. At the upper end, global poverty affects approximately 4.3 billion people (Hickel 2016: 17). David Woodward (2010) also suggested that an IPL of $5 a day would be a more realistic measure of poverty.

Lant Pritchett (2006) uses the Bank's 1985 base year ($1 a day) to construct a number of poverty lines, ranging from *destitute* (below $1 a day), to *extreme poor* (below $2 a day), to *global poor* (below $10 a day) and *not poor* (above $10 a day). He calculates that, in 2006, just under 88 per cent of the world's population lived in global poverty and just over 12 per cent of the world's population was 'not poor.' His $10-a-day poverty line – ten times that of the Bank (at its earlier $1-a-day poverty line) – appears radical only because of the latter's miserly level. But even such an apparently generous poverty line does not take into account the multidimensional aspects of poverty. As with the Bank's concern with the value of poor people's consumption, Pritchett's money-metric conception excludes non-income dimensions of poverty.

The way the $1-a-day IPL has been operationalised is inhuman. It is normatively bankrupt and undermines progressive thinking about, and strategies to achieve, genuine human development. A more societally sensitive absolute poverty line could, for example, be set according to living wage calculations. These would establish the costs of purchasing a basket of goods and services that are essential to achieving a *socially acceptable* standard of living. It would then investigate the extent to which household members, based upon the wages of their breadwinners, are able to consume these goods and services.[7]

A living wage calculation of poverty, in contrast to the Bank's elite-imposed definition, could be based upon workers' assessments of their minimum daily survival requirements – a social-relational conception of acceptable living standards. And, unlike the Bank's poverty line, it would link concerns about poverty to those about inequality, as the latter represents an important determinant of how poor and non-poor sections of the population see themselves and each other. It would, in short, entail taking the 'moral element' of poverty calculation as seriously as the physical element (see Marx [1867] 1990: 275).[8]

Such an alternative approach to measuring poverty is feasible and desirable, would catalyse a more thoroughgoing debate about how really to combat poverty, and would place class relations back at the centre of political economic analysis. But it is precisely for these reasons that such an approach would be resisted and rejected by the APC. Chapter 3 begins to illuminate how a poverty calculation based upon a living wage reveals that many workers who are assumed to be non-poor actually suffer from work-induced poverty.

Beyond poverty analysis: the rise of the developing world middle class

The APC's arguments about the developmentally beneficial effects of global capitalism have been extended further than its core claims about poverty reduction. Influential figures and institutions from across the political spectrum argue that this reduction is generating the emergence of a developing world middle class (DWMC). These arguments have been articulated by both the World Bank's Martin Ravallion (again) and the International Labour Organization (ILO) and have become part and parcel of the global development community's common sense.

Ravallion argues that, while in 1990 one-third of developing world country populations was middle class, by 2005 the proportion had risen to half. 'An extra 1.2 billion people joined the developing world's middle class over 1990–2005' (Ravallion 2010: 452). The ILO claims that, in 2011, over 40 per cent of workers were middle class and above and predicted that, by 2017, the figure would rise to over 50 per cent (Kapsos and Bourmpoula 2013).

Ravallion and the ILO adopt stratification conceptions of class, where it is defined according to aggregates of individuals consuming the same value of goods. They present class structure (as opposed to class relations) as a hierarchy that can be ascended through individual hard work and rising firm-level productivity (yielding higher wages), leading to rising incomes and more consumption. (The following chapter shows why these assumptions are wrong.) Such a *stratification-based* conception of class precludes, *a priori*, any meaningful investigation or theorisation of how *relations between classes* shape the livelihoods of the world's poor and non-poor populations.

In his assessment of what counts as middle class, Ravallion starts 'from the premise that middle class living standards begin where poverty ends' (2010: 446). He sets the value of consumption range of DWMC individuals at between $2 (2005 PPP) and $13 a day. $2 a day was the World Bank's upper poverty threshold under its previous international poverty line, and $13 a day was the US poverty line at the time Ravallion made these claims. The ILO, following Ravallion, albeit a little more generously, classifies DWMC individuals as consuming the equivalent of between $4 and $13 a day (2005 PPP) (Kapsos and Bourmpoula 2013: 4). A closer examination of Ravallion's point of departure, however, illuminates a failure of rhetoric and logic. His starting point, that 'middle class living standards begin where poverty ends', represents a tacit admission that working-class living standards equate to poverty. According to his logic, to be working class in developing countries is to be poor.

Arguments about the rising developing world middle class represent APC-charged doublethink. In 2013, the minimum wage of a Cambodian garment worker was $75 a month (in market exchange rates – i.e., much more than $75 per month PPP). Assuming that two parents, in a family of four, earned this minimum wage, then, according to Ravallion and the ILO, the family was middle class, because household per-capita consumption would be above $2 and $4 per capita, respectively. The Asian Floor Wage Alliance, however, estimates that a living wage – enough to provide for a family's basic needs – is $283 a month (in market exchange rates), almost four times the minimum wage.[9] Even if both parents within a family of four earn the minimum wage, the family will still be unable to meet its basic needs. And yet, according to Ravallion and the ILO, they are classified as middle class.

Even if it is assumed that Ravallion and the ILO's starting points are valid, the limitations of their arguments are transparent. Even an IPL of $10 a day does not fully guarantee an escape from poverty

(López-Calva and Ortiz-Juarez 2014; Sumner 2016: 6). The several billion people who live just above the World Bank's poverty line are prone to falling below it as a consequence of personal circumstances (such as ill health) and/or because of economic slowdown. To live above $2 or $4 PPP a day hardly denotes a middle-class social location. That 'the poor' are working class, according to Ravallion's logic, and that the so-called middle class are largely poor according to any reasonable calculation of poverty and are vulnerable to falling below the World Bank's inhumanly low poverty line, renders the claims of Ravallion and the ILO redundant.

Ravallion's methodology and its uptake by global institutions reveals a tacit recognition by APC proponents that capitalist globalisation is founded upon the proliferation of degrading work. Before the rise of neoliberal ideological hegemony, what most academics and informed commentators would have regarded as working-class jobs are now considered the preserve of the middle class. And those who are poor are now classified as working class.

Ravallion and the ILO's interpretations are somewhat undermined by more qualitative accounts of the DWMC. Abhijit Banerjee and Esther Duflo (2007) note, for example, that the DWMC's defining characteristic is a *steady, waged job*: Indian middle-class families' signs of affluence are to have a metal roof and send their children to secondary school. The journalist Paul Mason writes that being part of the DWMC 'means often living in a chaotic mega-city, cheek-by-jowl with abject poverty and crime, crowding on to makeshift public transport systems and seeing your income leach away into the pockets of all kinds of corrupt officials.'[10]

As will be shown in chapter 3, the expanding developing world middle class is better described as part of a burgeoning global labouring class. To be sure, while that class is far from uniform – in income, types of work, and living conditions – it does have something in common that Ravallion and the ILO ignore: the compulsion to sell its labour power in exchange for a wage and the exploitation by another social class. Only within APC discourse is being subject to such pressures described as 'graduating' to developing world middle-class status.

The following section moves beyond APC discourse and provides the basis for understanding why and how wealth and poverty are two sides of the same coin of capitalist development.

Capitalism, exploitation and poverty

The APC rejects the claim that capitalism is exploitative and poverty-generating. For example, the former UN Millennium project director Jeffrey Sachs discounts accusations that sweatshops are exploitative. Rather, he argues that they are 'the first rung on the ladder out of extreme poverty' and that 'rich-world protestors ... should support increased numbers of such jobs' (Sachs 2005: 11). Sachs's justification for such arguments is that workers in (many) sweatshops live at above the $1-a-day poverty line. As previously noted, however, this IPL is inhumanly low. A higher and more humane poverty line would show that sweatshop workers are experiencing new forms of poverty-inducing employment rather than poverty alleviation.

Sachs and other APC proponents draw upon arguments from neoclassical economics to scorn claims that capitalism is exploitative. Neoclassical economics holds that a transaction that leaves both actors better off than before (even if unevenly) is mutually beneficial and so cannot be exploitative. Legally binding contracts between freely consenting actors facilitate the mutually beneficial exchange of employment and wages in return for labour.

In his influential *Why Globalization Works,* Martin Wolf (2005: 183) explicitly rejects arguments that explain workers' poverty as a consequence of their exploitation by capital. In a tone and logic worthy of British tabloid newspapers, he argues that '[it] is right to say that transnational companies exploit their Chinese workers in the hope of making profits. It is equally right to say that Chinese workers are exploiting transnationals in the (almost universally fulfilled) hope of obtaining higher pay, better training and more opportunities.'

In contrast to the APC, this book argues that capitalism is a social system of exploitation, expropriation and degradation which generates continually evolving forms of poverty.

The particularity of capitalist exploitation

Capitalism is a social system organised around two core relations: endless competitive accumulation between units of capital (also referred to as 'firms', 'enterprises' or 'corporations') and the exploitation of labour by capital. Under capitalism, value is generated by workers' labour. The pool of total global wealth is fought over by firms, with each one trying to maximise its share.

As will be seen in chapter 3, contemporary transnational corporations have developed novel techniques to appropriate the lion's share of the wealth produced by globally dispersed labouring classes. Marx famously referred to the capitalist class as a band of 'hostile brothers' – hostile because they compete among themselves for the largest share of value, brothers because they are united in the exploitation of labour. The answer to the paradox of the simultaneous existence of vast global wealth and mass poverty must be sought with reference to these core social relations.

Within all class societies – from ancient Rome, to medieval

35

European feudalism, to contemporary global capitalism – labouring classes, whether slaves, peasants or wage labourers, have worked under the direction of a small minority of the population. The latter, whether slave-owners, feudal lords or managers of capitalist enterprises, have used various means (ranging from direct coercion to economic force) to extract wealth from the former. Under class societies labour can be conceived of as taking two forms – necessary and surplus labour. Necessary labour refers to labour required to produce the wealth for the reproduction of the workers and their families – their food, shelter, clothing and, under modern capitalism, perhaps health and educational provision. Surplus labour refers to that performed by labouring classes but expropriated by exploiting classes (Harman 1999).

Before capitalism, the appropriation of surplus labour took 'extra-economic' forms, such as the subjection of slaves and serfs to forced labour, or lords' seizure of peasants' produce. Capitalism is a unique form of class society because the appropriation of surplus labour takes place, largely, through economic means (Wood 1981). Under capitalism, surplus labour appropriation is 'invisible' because it occurs after the voluntary signing of a contract between worker and employer. Appropriated surplus labour takes the form of surplus value, which is the basis of capitalist profits. Within the workplace, the objective of capitalist employers is to reduce the amount of necessary labour and increase the amount of surplus labour performed by workers. This objective is supported by capitalist states (through the generation, allocation and defence of property rights) and justified ideologically in popular economic discourse (explained as raising labour productivity).

The capital–labour relation is the matrix through which contemporary dynamics of poverty and inequality are (re)produced and intensified. This is so in at least three ways. The capitalist enters into the direct (workplace-based) capital–labour relation as buyer of commodities in order to produce other commodities of greater value than those originally purchased. The worker enters the relation as holder of a single sellable commodity – labour power. Within production, labour power is combined with other inputs (such as machinery and raw materials) to generate new commodities. At the end of the production process the capitalist emerges with a commodity of greater value than that which they purchased initially. The worker emerges with a wage which is (sometimes) sufficient to reproduce the commodity initially sold to the capitalist – their labour power – through the purchase of other basic commodities (food, shelter, clothing).

For the capitalist, the relationship consists of M–C–M′, while for the worker it consists of C–M–C. The capitalist transforms money (M) into commodities (C) and then into a greater amount of money than their initial investment, or surplus value (M′). Workers, by contrast, sell their commodity of labour power (C) for a wage (M) which then enables them to purchase other commodities (basic goods) (C) to reproduce their labour power. At the end of the production process, the capitalist has increased the quantity of value at their disposal, while the worker has reproduced the commodity (labour power) which they sell to the capitalist. In production, workers' labour power generates more value than its initial cost to the capitalist – surplus value. This relation between capital and labour reproduces itself – as capitalists need to re-employ workers to secure continued production and workers need to find employment in order to earn the money to purchase goods to secure their social reproduction.

Second, endless competitive accumulation imposes productivity drives upon individual units of capital (firms): firms that fail to increase their productivity risk bankruptcy as other, more competitive firms appropriate their market share with more cheaply produced goods. Under capitalism, productivity drives are intended not to improve the living standards of workers but to cut costs, in particular wage costs. Increases in their productivity reduce workers' *relative wage* – the difference between the value (wages) that they retain and the value that they produce. The tendency towards polarisation of wealth which is intrinsic to the capital–labour relation is thus reinforced.

Third, rising productivity has an additional, polarising impact upon the capital–labour relationship. As fewer workers are required to produce the same amount of goods, and unless there is rapid expansion elsewhere in the economy, it is likely that productivity increases will generate rising unemployment and a situation where more workers are chasing fewer jobs. As Lucia Pradella (2015: 601) puts it: 'A greater labour supply . . . creates the conditions for a compression of wages, and the low level of wages pushes workers to prolong the working day [in order to earn the same as they did before wages fell], reducing the demand for labour-power, and permitting a greater labour supply in the market, in a vicious circle.'

How do rival firms attempt to maintain or raise their profitability to, or above, the sector-wide profit rate? They can do so in relation to other firms and in relation to their workers. In relation to each other, firms attempt to seek out new technologies, new markets, new sources of supply, and new ways of making things (Schumpeter 1987; Marx [1867] 1990). The first firm in the market to be able to identify and take advantage of these possibilities can reap super-profits – profits well above the sector-wide average – because they can cut costs while selling their product at the market rate.

Firms pursue a number of interlinked strategies to increase the surplus value created by workers.

- Increasing *relative surplus value* extraction through the intensification of the working day as a consequence of technological and managerial innovations and/or by means of reducing the costs of labour power. The former strategy concerns the introduction of new productivity-enhancing technologies and the management of the labour process to increase productivity within a given time-frame of the 'normal' working day (about eight hours in Northern countries, often over ten hours in Southern countries). The latter strategy concerns the reproduction of labour power outside the workplace. For example, if workers can purchase cheaper wage goods (including food and clothing), then the cost of reproducing their labour power falls, enabling firms to push down nominal wages (the amount of cash workers receive in exchange for their labour power).

- Increasing *absolute surplus value* through lengthening the working day without increasing wages proportionately.
- *Immiseration* through pushing down real wages.
- *Super-exploitation* through paying workers less than the costs of reproducing their labour power.

The social reproduction of capitalism

The previous analysis provides only the basic tenets of Marx's theory of exploitation. Some Marxists, however, limit their conception of capitalism and analysis of exploitation to the above processes only – the production and extraction of surplus value *in the workplace* (Cohen 1978; Brenner 1986; Mandel 2002; Warren and Sender 1980). In these – sometimes labelled 'productivist' – variants of Marxism, labouring classes are defined principally by their direct (work-based) relations to capital.[11]

The main problem with productivist comprehensions of capitalist social relations is that they take as given the existence of a ready-to-exploit wage-labour force. Such accounts, however, assume what needs to be explained – how the propertyless wage-labour force is reared, disciplined and prepared to sell itself to capital. As Marx noted, 'The maintenance and reproduction of the working class is, and must ever be, a necessary condition for the reproduction of capital' (Marx [1867] 1990: 718). A theory of capitalist exploitation cannot only consider what occurs in the workplace but must also explain the social reproduction of a society within which such a particular form of exploitation occurs. As Harry Cleaver (2000) argues, it is not only the factory that should be the focus of Marxian analysis but the 'social factory' – i.e., capitalist society as a whole.

Michael Lebowitz provides the basis of such a theory by arguing that capitalism is reproduced through two circuits (or moments) of production. The first is the circuit of production (where surplus value is produced by workers and appropriated by capitalists). The second is the circuit of the reproduction of labour power – i.e., the generation of a wage-labour force ready to sell itself to capital (Lebowitz 2003: 65). While these circuits are distinct – the former occurring within the workplace, the latter occurring within the household and community – they mutually constitute and presuppose each other. Such an analytical approach requires incorporating theoretically 'the value producing labor associated with the waged economy' and 'the domestic labor (typically performed by women) required to give birth to, feed and raise the current generation of workers, and the children who will comprise the future workforce (Ferguson 2008: 44). In addition, however, a social reproduction approach must incorporate analytically the environmental dimensions of capitalist social expansion. As Isabella Bakker and Stephen Gill write, social reproduction 'refers to both biological reproduction of the species (and indeed its ecological framework) and ongoing reproduction of . . . labor power. . . . [It] involves institutions, processes and social relations associated with the *creation and main-*

tenance of communities – and upon which, ultimately, all production and exchange rests' (2003: 17–18).

The following sub-sections delve deeper into ways in which gender, race and environmental dimensions of capitalism are constructed to facilitate its reproduction.

Gendering labour

From the emergence of capitalism to contemporary globalisation, the gendering of class relations has been a means to classify, segregate and downgrade specific forms of work performed by women (Mies 1998). With the emergence of capitalism, women's domestic work became devalued, while (initially mostly men's) labour in workplaces became organised through a market-based wage-labour system. As Sylvia Federici notes, 'In the new monetary regime [capitalism] only production-for-market was defined as value-creating activity, whereas the reproduction of the worker began to be considered as valueless from an economic viewpoint and even ceased to be considered as work.' She continues:

> The economic importance of the reproduction of labour-power carried out in the home, and its function in the accumulation of capital became invisible, being mystified as a natural vocation and labelled 'women's labour'. In addition, women were excluded from many waged occupations and, when they worked for a wage, they earned a pittance compared to the average male wage. (Federici 2004: 74–5)

The particularity of the capitalist labour market – where a wage-labour force must sell its labour power to capitalist employers – was generated over centuries through at least two mutually constitutive processes: first, the separation of the direct producers from the means of production and, second, the institutional differentiation of productive and reproductive spheres (Elson 1994: Acker 2004). As families lost control over productive property (land) and the labour process (work) to capitalist employers, they 'lost the capacity to coordinate productive and reproductive tasks' (Laslett and Brenner 1989: 386).

Women's domestic labour generates use values (the current and future generation of workers and their vendible labour power) which are then appropriated by capital in the labour market (Vogel 2013). Capital, however, pays only a small contribution (usually through regressive taxation) for the social production of workers.

The contribution of women's unpaid domestic labour to the reproduction and expansion of capitalist economies is substantial. For example, in South and South-East Asia in 1997, predominantly female unpaid work contributed the equivalent of between 43 and 48 per cent of GDP (Hoskyns and Rai 2007: 309). Comparably, in the early 1990s, as a percentage of GDP the value of unpaid women's housework was estimated at 23 per cent in the US and 33 per cent in India.[12]

In a notable study of South Africa's platinum mineworkers, Asanda Benya shows how women's unpaid labour represents an essential support for male miners' work:

Women in the parts of the informal settlement with no running water . . . [wake] up . . . between 2am and 4am daily, to get water for their male partners to bathe in before they go to work . . . An injured partner . . . requires attention and her time, and is her responsibility if he is not hospitalised. A missed production target affects her budget and a grumpy and exhausted partner comes home to her. Part of her service is to uplift and encourage him. (Benya 2015: 552, 549, 550)

The gendering of society devalues women's *and* men's work. In their study of female participation in the Latin American labour force, Hite and Viterna show that women's employment in the (what is often portrayed as privileged) formal sector has increased rapidly since the 1980s. This increase is celebrated by the anti-poverty consensus, but Hite and Viterna highlight how it rests upon new dynamics of impoverishment:

> Women's increasing parity with men in terms of class position did not come from women's improving conditions . . . but rather from men 'falling down' the class ladder. Similarly, increasing income parity did not come from women's gains as much as it did from male workers' more rapid, intense impoverishment. (2005: 77)

Racism

Racism contributed to the rise of capitalism and continues to degrade, to devalue and to divide labouring classes among themselves. Capitalist classes and states have generated racial categories to organise large flows of workers from one part of the world to another and their employment/exploitation under dire conditions. From the Atlantic slavery of the seventeenth and eighteenth centuries, to the colonial 'coolie labour' system, to the globally integrated system of precarious migrant labour – racism de-politicises and naturalises the suffering of these sections of the global labouring class and provides an ultra-cheap pool of labour for capital to exploit (Ferguson and McNally 2015).

Racism is reproduced and marshalled to facilitate the reproduction of capitalism in at least three ways (Camfield 2016). First, it legitimates imperialism – a globally organised system of hierarchy and structural inequality. Contemporary imperialism 'correlates very well with racial criteria: the darker your skin is, the less you earn; the shorter your lifespan, the poorer your health and nutrition, the less education you get' (Winant 2004: 134–5, cited in Camfield 2016: 58–9). Second, racism reduces the potential for labouring-class solidarity within and beyond the workplace. It also reduces particular ethnic/racial groups to lower-status/lower-paid workers. Third, racism can be used as an organising category by better-off workers to defend their relatively privileged position in the labour force against worse-off workers – as a form of what W. E. B. Du Bois ([1935] 2103) referred to as 'psychological capital'.

Under contemporary global capitalism, racism is a particularly useful mechanism for core economies that rely to a large extent on incoming migrant labour, as it lowers the costs of these workers. As Susan Ferguson and David McNally argue:

> Migrant workers' transnational households and networks, and the state policies supporting these, institutionalize dramatically lower costs of social reproduction. Capital and the state in North America regularly draw from a pool of effectively 'cost free' labour power on whose past social reproduction they have not spent a dime. And because they deny or restrict migrant access to state resources and services, receiving nations also invest comparatively little in the current migrant workforce's ongoing regeneration. (2015: 12)

The APC's exercise in poverty accounting represents a form of globally articulated racism, as it is based upon and institutes a double standard in assessing the needs of populations in poor countries (biologically determined poverty lines) and rich countries (socially determined poverty lines) respectively. It justifies the continuing degradation of vast sections of the world's population by ideologically camouflaging their poverty and presenting it as development.

Externalising and commodifying nature

Capitalism expands through the appropriation of natural wealth. Since the emergence of capitalism in the sixteenth century, the natural environment has been socially constructed as a free or very cheap resource through which capital operates, by virtue of providing inputs into production and being a dumping ground for waste products. Under capitalism, 'nature' is simultaneously commodified (transformed into something to be bought and sold) and externalised (where its use and destruction are either not incorporated as a cost into capitalist production or are done so very cheaply) (Moore 2015).

The incorporation and subordination of the natural environment to the dynamics and requirements of capital accumulation could only occur through the seizure of land from the direct producers. In Britain this took place through the enclosure movement. In the colonial system it occurred through the 'extirpation, enslavement, and entombment in mines of the indigenous population' (Marx [1867] 1990: 915). The effects of the natural environment's subordination to capital accumulation are dire: global warming, devastating droughts, water shortages, melting glaciers, rising ocean levels, extinction of species, acidification of oceans, pollution of air and water, pesticides in water and food, ozone depletion, decline in biodiversity, soil erosion, deforestation, and exhaustion of finite non-renewable resources (Magdoff and Foster 2010). The poverty-inducing and life-threatening consequences of disasters caused by climate change, such as droughts and floods, are mounting. According to conservative estimates, during the 1990s, approximately 1 million people were killed by such disasters and around 200 million were pauperised (Harriss-White 2006).

Far from representing a barrier to further capitalist expansion, environmental disasters and risk can be made profitable. Carbon markets, pollution permits, climate derivatives and catastrophe bonds all generate new profit opportunities for financial investors (Keucheyan 2016).

The emergence of capitalist industry was enabled by a new society–nature matrix, in particular the discovery and use of new energy sources. Fossil energy – coal, petroleum and natural gas – facilitates rapid capitalist industrial expansion in a number of ways. It de-links production from the local availability of energy resources (for example, water or large wood stocks). The establishment, as part of the industrial revolution, of a network of means to deliver energy resources – canals, roads, railways – facilitated an ever-greater spatial expansion of industry. In addition, and in contrast to solar radiation, which varies by season and by day and night, fossil fuels can be used 24 hours a day, 365 days a year. The latter also enable capital to control and discipline labour more fully – as seasonal customs that alter working practices are reformed (Altvater 2007: 41; Malm 2016).

Fossil-fuel industrialisation has underpinned an ever-greater 'compression of time and space' through technological advance (Harvey 1996). This dialectic has been driven forward by new and ever more energy-intensive technologies (from motor cars to aeroplanes) and the development of an increasing range of productivity-raising industrial inputs.

While humans' appropriation of nature's wealth is as old as humanity itself, under capitalism the scale of this appropriation is qualitatively different to anything that went before. 'All progress in capitalist agriculture', wrote Marx, 'is a progress in the art, not only of robbing the worker, but of robbing the soil' (Marx [1867] 1990: 638).

Before the advent of capitalist agriculture farming was predominantly small-scale and determined by local ecology. Capitalist agriculture has increasingly broken apart the previously unified process of production – as land, labour and inputs were commodified – and producers became increasingly market-dependent. This process was dialectically related to the rise of agricultural science and, later on, the rise of productivity-enhancing agro-industry (Lievens 2010: 9). Capitalist agriculture is a major contributor to climate change and global environmental degradation, contributing directly to mass deforestation. For example, between 2000 and 2012, 71 per cent of tropical deforestation was caused by clearance for cultivation (Jones: 2014). Further, capitalist agriculture is reliant upon intensive fossil-fuel use (from pesticides and fertilisers to the machines that apply them) (Epsom 2016).

Despite productivity enhancements in agriculture through rising chemical inputs, the core contradiction of the contemporary global agricultural system – of food shortages, malnutrition and starvation in the context of food over-abundance – is continually reproduced (McMichael 2009).[13] Not only does capitalist agriculture fail to feed the world's population but, through its reliance upon fossil-fuel-based inputs, it contributes directly to the globe's escalating environmental crisis (Weis 2007: 58).

Conclusions

The anti-poverty consensus has generated a powerful common-sense ideology about the measurement of, and means of combating, global poverty. It uses data generated by an inhumanly low international poverty line to claim that millions of people across the globe are getting out of poverty and, consequently, entering the middle class. Poverty analysis based upon living wage calculations would show that the majority of the world's population live in poverty.

The APC discourse is designed to preclude any serious discussion of the relationship between capitalism and poverty. It does this by presenting capitalism as a sphere of developmental opportunity where individuals are free to engage in mutually beneficial exchange. It rejects any attempt to consider how class relations are exploitative and how they are the root cause of the two-sided nature of capitalist development – expanding wealth and mass poverty.

This chapter also presented an outline of Marx's conception of capitalist exploitation. It showed how, while exploitation under capitalism occurs within the workplace, the social reproduction of exploitative class relations rests upon a variety of forms of appropriation – from women's unpaid domestic labour, to nature's 'free gifts' to capital, to the use of racism to devalue and degrade large sections of the world's labouring class.

The following chapter employs these theoretical tools to investigate the relationship between expanding global supply chains and a proliferating and impoverished global labouring class.

Poverty Chains and the World Economy

Introduction

One of the core claims of the anti-poverty consensus is that global integration – through foreign investment, trade, and export-orientated production – generates faster growth and poverty reduction and is the swiftest route to human development. The global value chain (GVC) concept has emerged in academia and spread into the policy mainstream as a theoretical-policy expression of these claims.[1] From the World Bank, to UNCTAD, to the OECD, to the WTO, GVC analysis is everywhere. For example, the secretary general of the Organisation for Economic Cooperation and Development, Angel Gurría, recently stated that 'everyone can benefit from global value chains . . . [and] we will all benefit more if governments take steps to enhance the new business environment . . . [Furthermore,] encouraging the development of and participation in global value chains is the road to more jobs and sustainable growth for our economies' (cited in Werner et al. 2014: 1220).

This chapter argues, by contrast, that workers in these chains (who are predominantly women of colour) are systematically paid less than their subsistence costs, that transnational corporations use their global market power to capture the lion's share of value created within these chains, and that these relations generate processes of immiserating (poverty-inducing) growth (Smith 2016 makes a similar argument).[2] For these reasons it argues for labelling GVCs as global poverty chains (GPCs). It shows, furthermore, how GPCs operate through environmental degradation.

Firms' survival in capitalist markets is dependent upon their ability to match or sustain sector-wide profitability. If they cannot do so, they will be unable to raise sufficient funds to invest as much as their competitors and will eventually be outcompeted and forced out of business. How do rival firms attempt to maintain or raise their profitability to, or above, the sector-wide profit rate? As noted in chapter 2, they can do so in relation to other firms and in relation to their workers.

The great Austrian political economist Joseph Schumpeter (1987) identified how, in relation to each other, firms seek out new technologies, new markets, new sources of supply, and new ways of making things. If they are the first firm in the market to identify and take advantage of these possibilities, they can reap super-profits – well above the sector-wide average – through cutting costs while selling their product at the market rate. These innovative drives and practices are given pride of place within GVC analysis, as representing forms of upgrading.

But such strategies are only one side of coin of capitalist competition. The other is (strict) labour management. Indeed, as discussed in chapter 2, the 'inner secret', as Marx ([1867] 1990) put it, of capitalist profit is capital's ability to reap a greater portion of value from workers' labour power (surplus value) than the cost of its initial purchase. Firms can increase the surplus value appropriated from workers through increasing rates of (a) relative surplus value extraction (intensification of the working day); (b) absolute surplus value extraction (lengthening the working day); (c) immiseration (by pushing down wages); or (d) super-exploitation (presiding over a labour regime where wages do not satisfy workers' subsistence requirements). One of the core arguments of this chapter is that the global manufacturing system is founded upon the generation of a vast, gendered and super-exploited labouring class.

That highly gendered and exploitative capital–labour relations have underpinned the proliferation of global poverty chains is observable in three ways. First, the predominance of women workers in globally integrated systems of production suggests that this form of industrialisation is as much 'female led as . . . export led' (Joekes 1987; Dunaway 2014).

Second, the increased 'feminisation' of the global labour force does not simply denote a higher percentage of women workers. Feminisation of labour refers to a dual process. Initially, women are employed by firms because of their perceived 'nimble fingers' – their ability to work long hours performing relatively complex tasks under harsh management – and their lack of political activism (Elson and Pearson 1981). Their employment conditions are usually poor, with limited rights. As Alessandra Mezzadri (2016: 1881) puts it, women workers are employed in these industries because they have 'a lower "price-tag" stuck to their body' (see also Bair 2010). Subsequently, however, male workers are (re-)employed under the 'feminised' conditions associated with women's work – of insecurity, low and irregular pay, casualisation and, above all, being subject to high rates of exploitation (Standing 1989; Sklair 1993).

Third, the burden of women's unpaid reproductive labour is intensified following their employment, as the latter 'has not been matched by an increased participation of men in unpaid domestic work' (Pearson 2000: 228; Ramamurthy 2004).

The remainder of this chapter is organised as follows. Section 3.2

provides an account of the global manufacturing system and its basis in and contribution to global wage differentiation. Section 3.3 examines workers' conditions in three sectors – textiles, food and high-tech. In each of these sectors, workers are primarily female. In some (food and some textiles production) they are predominantly young, in others (other parts of the global textile sector) they are middle-aged. In the former, these young women's livelihoods are subsidised or supported by their families (that is, by the unpaid labour of older women, including mothers, siblings and more distant family members). In the latter, middle-aged women also bear the brunt of the double burden of supporting a household. In each case, however, workers need to put in many hours of overtime to earn a subsistence wage.

The global manufacturing system

In *The End of the Third World*, Nigel Harris argued that the emerging global manufacturing system represented the end of the 'classical' division of labour where Northern countries produced and exported manufactured goods and imported primary goods from the South. He argued that 'The process of dispersal of manufacturing capacity brings enormous hope to areas where poverty has hitherto appeared immovable, and makes possible new divisions of labour and specializations which will vastly enhance the capacity of the world to feed everyone' (Harris 1987: 202). It is notable that neither Harris nor the vast majority of global value chain analysis stops to consider the centrality of the dispossession of the peasantry in the construction of the global manufacturing system. This dispossession provided land for new export crops, export processing zones, and vast sources of very cheap labour.

The formation of geographically dispersed, functionally integrated global value chains, 'governed' (coordinated and organised) by lead firms, represents the outcome of a successful attempt by these firms and their predecessors, supported by states and international institutions, to escape the core economy profit crisis of the 1970s. A central reason for (re)locating production in new, previously non-industrialised regions is low wage costs. As Charles Whalen (2005: 35) notes, 'The prime motivation behind offshoring is the desire to reduce labor costs. . . . a U.S.-based factory worker hired for $21 an hour can be replaced by a Chinese factory worker who is paid 64 cents an hour.'

The transport, logistics and information technology revolutions enabled simultaneous global dispersal and ever-closer functional integration of firms' activities. Within the contemporary global manufacturing system, Southern countries produce a voluminous range of industrial inputs and outputs, including fabricated metal goods, electronics equipment, chemicals, transport equipment, furniture and a whole range of textiles, in addition to agricultural products and extractive materials (UNIDO 2011).

The global manufacturing structure of world trade is increasingly intra-firm, between affiliates of the same corporation located in different countries. Around one-third of world trade is intra-firm (Lanz and Miroudot 2011). The percentage of world trade that occurs between nominally independent supplier firms and lead firms is often higher: '90 per cent of US exports and imports flow through a US TNC, with roughly 50 per cent of US trade flows occurring between affiliates of the same TNC' (Dicken 2011: 20–1).

TNCs derive an increasing share of their profits from overseas activities. Foreign affiliates accounted for approximately 17 per cent of US TNCs' worldwide net income in 1977, 27 per cent in 1994 and 48.6 per cent by 2006 (Slaughter 2009: 16). Rates of return on foreign investment have been 'consistently higher in developing countries (5.8%) than in developed (4.4%) and CEE [Central and Eastern European] countries (3.9%) since the beginning of the 1990s' (UNCTAD 2003:17). US TNCs occupy the pinnacle (and, through chain governance, actively contribute to the management) of the global wealth–poverty hierarchy. As Sean Starrs documents: 'American companies have the leading profit-shares among the world's top 2,000 firms in eighteen of twenty-five sectors, and a dominant position in ten – especially those at the technological frontier. In a reflection of this global hegemony, two fifths of the world's millionaire households are American' (Starrs 2014: 95). The global manufacturing system is, in short, a structure through which lead firms seek to enhance their global positions and strategies for extended capital accumulation and profit maximisation in relation to supplier firms, would-be competitor firms, and labouring classes.

The global business revolution

Lead firms govern global supply chains by establishing and imposing a range of requirements upon supplier firms – including product specifications, production conditions, delivery times and, most significantly, price. Lead firms have concentrated increasingly upon their 'core competencies' – areas where they possess or can establish a competitive advantage vis-à-vis other lead firms and/or where they can establish powerful relations over supplier firms. These strategies enable lead firms to outsource risks and costs of production and supply and to preside, at a distance, over heightened labour exploitation. They also enhance their ability to capture value from other actors within the chain (Smith 2012).

TNCs began pursuing the global business revolution in the 1980s and 1990s through increasing spending on research and development, branding, and high investments in IT and related services, and through a 'merger frenzy' (Nolan 2003: 302-3). In the mid-2000s the world's top 1,400 (the G1,400) firms invested US$445 billion in research and development. The top 100 firms 'account for 60 per cent of the total R&D spending of the G1,400, while the bottom 100 firms account for less than 1 per cent of the total' (Nolan 2014: 750).

A consequence of lead firms' concentration on core competencies has been a 'cascade effect' across industrial sectors, generating intense pressure upon first- and then second-tier suppliers to merge, acquire and themselves follow TNCs' strategies. According to Peter Nolan:

> Large capitalist firms now stand at the centre of a vast network of outsourced businesses which are highly dependent on the core system integrators for their survival. The system integrators possess the technology and/or brand name which indirectly provides sales to the supplier firms. They are therefore able to ensure that [they] obtain the lion's share of the profits from the transactions between the two sets of firms. (Nolan 2003: 317-18)

As part of the process of centralising their economic power, '"monopso-nistic" buyer[s] [can] . . . push down the prices of supplies to marginal cost and thus extract the full profits from the sales of the final goods from a smaller capital stake' (Strange and Newton 2006: 184). William Milberg calls this the 'mark-up effect . . . [through] which the lead firm in the global value chain is able to raise the mark-up over costs, not in the traditional oligopoly fashion of raising product prices, but through the control of input costs' (Milberg 2008: 429). For example, significant import price declines (of over 40 per cent between 1986 and 2006) have benefited US firms engaged in computers, electrical and telecom-munications products, clothing, footwear, textiles, furniture, chemicals and miscellaneous manufactures (including toys) (ibid.: 433).

The global business revolution and wage rate determination

The APC and mainstream GVC discourse maintains that workers' low wages reflect their employment in low-productivity economic sectors (e.g., Taglioni and Winkler 2014). Economists in the Employment Trends Unit of the International Labour Office contend, for example, that 'poverty should be less associated with employment in a higher-productivity economy', and that, 'As higher levels of productivity facilitate higher average earnings from labour, there is a direct link between labour market outcomes – in terms of both the quantity of available jobs and the productivity of the workforce – and the middle class standard of living enjoyed by the majority of people in the developed world' (Kapsos and Bourmpoula 2013: 12, 1). In more popular terms, Martin Wolf (2005: 175) maintains that 'the evidence on the [proportionate] relationship between productivity and wages is overwhelming.'

The policy implications of the above arguments are to prioritise enhancing firm-level competitiveness over increasing workers' rights and wages. It portrays firm-level upgrading from the perspective of capital and encourages workers to do the same. But these assumptions are based neither on lucid theory nor on substantial evidence.

APC-type arguments that low wages in poor countries reflect low productivity levels are simplistic and, in some ways, fundamentally erroneous.[3] First, they fail to differentiate between national average productivity and the productivity of firms integrated into dynamic global value chains. It is likely that national average productivity in poor countries will be lower than that in rich countries because of the former's relatively large subsistence agriculture and small-scale, mostly low-tech industrial sectors. However, the opposite is the case in large high-tech export-orientated firms. In such workplaces, lead firms require suppliers to adopt advanced technologies to meet world market quality requirements at low cost. Here, worker productivity may be comparable to if not higher than that in similar firms in rich countries, while their pay may be ten, twenty or thirty times less than that of workers in rich countries (Whalen 2005).

Second, the productivity–wage relation is primarily determined not by firm-level productivity but by labour's social reproduction costs and by the balance of power between capital and labour. Where social reproduction costs are low, and where states have instituted a capital–labour relation where workers are dependent on excessive overtime and/or other sources of wage supplements to generate a living wage, then, regardless of productivity, firms will find it relatively easy to pay workers poverty wages.

Third, APC arguments assume that workers are rewarded according to the value they produce. But, as noted above, capitalists seek continually to maximise surplus value by extracting as much surplus labour as possible from workers.

There is much data to support these arguments. In the 1990s, for example, Doug Henwood (1995: 33) showed how US firms in the Mexican maquila sector were 85 per cent as productive as their US-based counterparts, but paid their workers only 6 per cent of the wages of the US-based workers undertaking comparable tasks. Tony Norfield (2012) writes about Foxconn that its 'level of technology is not so different from that which would be available in the home country, but the conditions of labour exploitation are certainly far more extreme than in the home country.' Similarly, Robert Wade (2008: 380) notes that, for undertaking essentially the same work, 'the best-paid bus drivers in the world get thirty times the real wages of the worst-paid.'

Productivity can be measured by dividing the output of a productive

Table 3.1 Country productivity ranking (automobiles and textiles)

Country	Year	Value added per worker (annual US$)	Wages per worker (annual US$)	Average productivity (US$) $value added/$wages
Automobiles				
Mexico	2000	102,000	11,700	8.69
India	2003	22,817	4,575	4.99
US	2002	231,729	54,157	4.28
Thailand	2000	13,555	4,680	2.85
Germany	2003	89,117	56,425	1.58
Textiles				
Brazil	2004	12,353	3,584	3.45
Thailand	2000	6,583	2,318	2.84
Mexico	2000	14,983	5,292	2.83
US	2002	66,483	27,223	2.44
Germany	2003	43,881	30,974	1.42

Source: UNIDO (2006), adapted from Kerswell (2013: 513).

process by its input. Table 3.1 provides calculations of productivity in autos and textiles in the early 2000s by value (dividing worker value added in US$ by their average salary). It shows that Mexico and India had higher productivity rates than the US and Germany in autos, and that Brazil, Thailand and Mexico had higher productivity rates than the US and Germany in textiles (Kerswell 2013). The implication is that barriers to enhancing workers' wages and conditions are not low productivity but (supplier and lead) firm profit-maximisation strategies.[4]

While more research is undoubtedly needed on productivity–wage relationships, it is credible to argue that wage rates reflect less in-firm productivity levels than (at least a combination of) (1) the socially determined costs of wage-labour force reproduction, (2) labour market institutions (that do or do not seek to link wage rates to productivity) and (3) the ability of labouring-class organisations to achieve 'progressive' wage settlements (Moseley 2008). Where the first variable is very low, the second (often purposely) pro-capital, and the third weak, and where firms utilise relatively advanced technologies, they can benefit from higher productivity levels than those in core economies, which can facilitate increasing value extraction and appropriation (see Ali 2016).

Global poverty chains: three case studies

This section provides empirical examples of labour conditions, wages, and socially determined reproduction costs in global poverty chains in three globally orientated industries. In doing so, it advances three core arguments. First, lead firms use their market power to capture the lion's share of the value created in each chain. Second, employment in these industries does not represent 'the first rung on the ladder out of extreme poverty' (Sachs 2005: 11) but, on the contrary, generates new forms of poverty. Third, lead firms, in conjunction with local firms and states, play a significant part in generating these poverty-inducing conditions, designed to facilitate their value-capture strategies.

Textiles

Approximately 30 million workers are employed in the fast-expanding global garment industry (Luginbühl and Musiolek 2014: 28). There are regular media reports about abusive working conditions in these industries, ranging from extremely low pay to child and forced labour. Most horrifically, in Bangladesh in April 2013, 1,113 garment workers were killed and 2,500 injured following the collapse of Rana Plaza, an eight-storey building in which textile factories operated.

Women workers predominate in this industry. In their analysis of Bangladeshi export garment industries, Kabeer and Mahmud (2004: 108) argue that 'employers regard their female workforce as dispensable labour to be exploited ruthlessly for a period of time and then replaced by the apparently unlimited supply of young women flowing in from the countryside in search of such work.' In his overview of the apparel sector across seventeen countries, John Pickles (2012: 105) documents how, from the mid-2000s onwards, 'wage levels were driven below subsistence costs.'

The extent of retailer (lead-firm) power in the garment industry is illustrated by table 3.2, which disaggregates the sale price of a T-shirt made in Bangladesh and sold in Germany by H&M for €4.95 (Norfield 2012, 2014). Norfield estimates that the average labour cost to produce one T-shirt is between 2 and 3 cents and reports that 'One worker at the factory, even after a 17% pay rise, earned just 1.36 euros per day based on a 10–12 hour day. The machine she works with produces a target of 250 T-shirts per hour' (2014: 1).

Large-scale export-orientated textile production has been established across Cambodia. It began producing garments for export in the 1990s following state-sponsored subsidies to overseas capital (comprising tax holidays and duty-free imports of machinery and material) and bilateral trade agreements with the US, the EU and Canada. In 2014 its garment exports totalled approximately $5.7 billion. The majority of factories engage in 'cut-and-trim' activities – producing clothes with imported textiles and designs provided by global buyers.

Table 3.2 T-shirt sale price disaggregation

€0.40	Cost of 400g of cotton raw material bought from the US by the factory in Bangladesh
€1.35	Price H&M paid per T-shirt to the Bangladeshi company
€1.41	After adding €0.06 per shirt for shipping costs to Hamburg, Germany
€3.40	After adding some €2 for transport in Germany, shop rent, sales force, marketing and administration
€4.16	After adding €0.60 net profit of H&M plus some other items
€4.95	After adding 19% VAT, paid to the German state

Source: Norfield (2012).

Factories vary in size, ranging from those employing more than 8,000 workers to small-scale home-based production units. Women make up over 90 per cent of the workforce. In 2014 Cambodia's garment sector employed more than 700,000 workers (excluding those based at home) (Human Rights Watch 2015).

Within Cambodia's garment industry, the labour process is intense and characterised by continual productivity drives. Employment rights are minimal. Employers require workers to meet very high daily task targets. For example, they must produce 1,200 'difficult design' and 2,000 'simple design' garments in an eleven-hour shift. Workers are subject to tight surveillance. As one testified: 'We cannot go to the toilet when we want. If we go three times during the day it is considered too much. They announce it on the speaker: "Don't go to the toilet. You cannot produce a lot and meet your targets. You need to sew faster"' (Human Rights Watch 2015: 62). Working conditions are so harsh that workers regularly faint as a consequence of the intensity of labour required of them (Arnold 2013; McMullen 2013). Overtime is a necessity for most workers, as their regular wages are insufficient to meet their daily needs (table 3.3). While the government limits overtime to two hours per day, this is not legally enforced. Most workers in the large Cambodian textile factories work between three and five hours overtime a day (Human Rights Watch 2015: 58).

These dynamics have generated numerous strikes and protests by workers, which have met with brutal state responses. For example, in December 2013 the Labour Ministry announced an increase in the minimum wage from $80 to $100 per month, effective from February 2014. Workers responded by holding large-scale demonstrations demanding a $160 minimum wage, citing a tripartite (government, industry and trade union) report recommending a living wage of between $157 and $177. The state's response to workers' protests was severe:

Table 3.3 Legal minimum wage vs living wage: Eastern Europe and Asia compared

Eastern Europe (including Turkey)	Minimum wage as a percentage of living wage	Asia	Minimum wage as a percentage of living wage
Slovakia	21	India	26
Ukraine	14	China	46
Romania	19	Bangladesh	19
Moldova	19	Cambodia	21
Georgia	10	Malaysia	54
Bosnia and Herzegovina	25	Sri Lanka	19
Macedonia	14	Indonesia	31
Bulgaria	14		
Croatia	36		
Turkey	28		

Source: Luginbühl and Musiolek (2014: 34).

On the morning of January 3, the authorities sent a large force of gendarmes to seize control of the area, some of whom fired their assault rifles towards the crowds, killing six people. A person beaten by gendarmes later died of his injuries. Twenty-three human rights defenders and workers arrested during these incidents were later charged with responsibility for the violence, tried and convicted, and sentenced to prison terms, despite there being no evidence against them. Their sentences were all suspended, but they remain at risk of imprisonment. No gendarmes were prosecuted. (Human Rights Watch 2015: 40)

It is not only the workforces in formerly 'Third World' countries that suffer from the dynamics of immiserating growth. Across a number of post-socialist countries, and in Turkey, approximately 3 million workers labour in the garment industry.[5] The main export markets are Germany and Italy. These wages represent the principal livelihood of approximately 9 million people (workers and dependants). The workers are predominantly young and middle-aged women, and they are subject to similar productivity-based pressures to those in Cambodian factories.

Wages received by workers in the garment industries of Eastern Europe and Turkey are often even lower, as a ratio of the living wage, than those received by workers in East Asia (table 3.3). Consequently, workers cannot live on their wages alone. As one Turkish worker said, 'If we only depended on our wages, we would starve to death' (Luginbühl and Musiolek 2014: 38).

How then, do workers and their families survive on poverty wages? Many workers and their extended families cultivate subsistence agriculture to subsidise their wages and save on food costs. Employers in a number of the Eastern European countries studied by the Clean Clothes Campaign (CCC) 'build factories in rural areas where people are clearly engaging in agriculture and thus have additional income.' Other survival strategies include working overtime – up to twenty hours a week. Debt and eliminating any family expenditure on 'non-emergency' health services, heating and school supplies, limiting travel, buying only the cheapest foods and second-hand clothes, and stealing electricity represent other survival strategies (Luginbühl and Musiolek 2014: 44, 45). In its survey of garment industry workers, the CCC concludes that, in Eastern and South Eastern Europe, 'Just like in Asia, the legal minimum wages are poverty wages. In all researched countries . . . the legal minimum wage is set far below a subsistence minimum . . . . The legal minimum wage . . . consolidates poverty rather than eliminating it' (ibid.: 30).

Food and agriculture

The production, distribution and consumption of food has been transformed over the last four decades. For an increasing number of food commodities, production is orientated towards sale for profit in distant markets rather than being for self- or local consumption.

Philip McMichael (2000) characterises this transformation as the dismantling of 'national food regimes' and agriculture's upward integration into new circuits of globalised capital. National food regimes, designed by nation-states to feed their populations after 1945, were dismantled from the 1980s onwards. They were replaced with increasingly globally orientated agricultural systems designed to earn foreign exchange to pay off combinations of debt and structural adjustment loans. Rapidly concentrating retail capital (first Northern, now increasingly Southern) has engaged in a 'retail revolution' based on new systems of procurement and the integration into supply chains of producers from newly established agricultural zones (Reardon et al. 2003). States across the global South facilitated this transformation through the 'modernisation' of agriculture – introducing high-tech machinery to displace labour and raise existing labour's productivity, stimulating the use of a wide range of chemical inputs (from fertilisers to pesticides) and high-yield crops. In Brazil, for example, under the post-1964 military regime's programme of 'conservative modernisation', more than 30 million workers were expelled from the rural sector between the 1960s and the 1980s (Welch 2006).

Across Latin America, new sub-sectors producing non-traditional agricultural exports (NTAXs) have boomed. These include cut flowers from Ecuador, wine and fruits from Chile, peanuts from Nicaragua, winter vegetables from Peru, Mexico and Guatemala, and soy from Argentina and Brazil. NTAXs have transformed the countryside across

Latin America through (1) the increasing dominance of local agricultural systems by transnational capital, (2) the displacement of the peasantry and its conversion into a rural proletariat, (3) the use of casualised work practices by employers, (4) the predominance of women workers in NTAX sectors, and (5) 'the articulation of local agricultural systems to the global supermarket' (Robinson 2008: 58).

Giant retailers such as WalMart, Carrefour and Tesco have occupied centre-stage in the globalised food system. Mega-retailers now stock a vast range of fresh fruits and vegetables, cultivated from across the globe, available fifty-two weeks of the year, and produced according to strict retailer requirements. These requirements govern the shape, size, colour, sugar-content levels, quantity, timing of delivery, and types of packaging which exporters must meet if they are to sell to global retailers. The global retail revolution has been both cause and effect of a long-term process of retail market concentration. For example, the combined market share of the four largest US grocery retailers rose from 14 per cent in 1984 to around 55 per cent in 2001 (Swinnen and Vandeplas 2010: 111).

The above-noted requirements, in addition to continual cost-down pressures, can be imposed upon producers because the latter compete aggressively with each other to supply retailers. Northern retailers and importers have enjoyed long-term falling cost prices. For example, in the US, between 1986 and 2006, the *average annual percentage* change in import prices for beverages, fruit, vegetables and nuts, and meats and fish fell by 0.41, 0.58, 0.62 and 0.91 per cent, respectively (Milberg 2008: 432).

The power of global retail capital, and its ability to capture the lion's share of value from agricultural production, was illustrated by Conroy and his colleagues' study of melon production in El Salvador in the relatively early stages of the global retail revolution (table 3.4). In 1991, while a pound of Salvadorian melon retailed in the United States for

Table 3.4 Distribution of value in the melon chain (percentages)

US shipping and retailing	76.6
International shippers	9.1
Imported inputs	5.1
US brokers	2.6
Packer and exporter profits	2.5
Miscellaneous in-country services	3.5
Farmer profits	0.6

Source: Conroy et al. (1996: 105–7).

65 cents, only about half a cent contributed to the farmer's income, of which workers received only a fraction (Conroy et al. 1996: 105–7).

Similarly, in the UK during the two periods 1975 to 1989 and 2000 to 2009, the import price of coffee fell from an average of 43 per cent to 14 per cent of its retail price (Seudieu 2011). One study estimates that coffee cultivators receive less than 2 per cent of the final retail price (Oxfam 2002). As Daviron and Ponte (2005) argue, the 'coffee paradox' of the late twentieth and early twenty-first century was sky-rocketing prices paid by Northern consumers for coffee beverages and the falling prices received by coffee bean farmers.

Under the Pinochet dictatorship, Chile become a mass producer of fresh fruits and vegetables, such as table grapes, and shifted from producing traditional agricultural crops to wine grapes (Gwynne 1999). By 2013, its agro-exports earned US$11.6 billion, and Chile is often represented as a poster-child of neoliberal market-led growth.

During the table grape-sector harvest period, approximately 700,000 (mostly women) workers are employed to pick and pack the fruit for export. Wages have been stagnant since the 1980s as a consequence of the purposeful construction of a low-wage labour regime by Pinochet and his followers (Clark 2015). Alicia Muñoz, director of the National Rural and Indigenous Women's Association, describes how women 'break their backs doing double shifts [approximately sixteen hours a day], to earn US$ 800 or 1,000 a month.'[6] Consequently, 'we have disposable workers, who as a result of exhaustion and the effects of pesticides are sick and unable to work by the age of 40 or 50.' Most of the women workers are also heads of household, thus enduring a particularly tough double burden.

Brazilian sugar-cane production around São Paulo has boomed in response to rising bio-fuel demand and, through industrial restructuring, has become increasingly capital-intensive since the early 2000s. Despite significant productivity increases, however, workers receive three times less than the necessary wage to meet their living needs (Garvey et al. 2015: 88).

In 2014, Mexico's export berry harvest was worth approximately US$550 million. Workers, who pick strawberries and other fruits for export to the US, receive 110 pesos (US$7) for ten-hour working days with no overtime pay.[7] David Bacon (2015) describes the living conditions of one of the Mexican fruit pickers, Claudia Reyes (whose name has been changed to protect her identity):

Reyes' home in Santa Maria de Los Pinos is a cinderblock house with a concrete floor, an amenity many neighbors lack. Several years after building it she still can't come up with the money to buy frames and glass panes for windows. She's also strung electrical conduit and plugs up the concrete walls, but the government provides no electrical service. 'We buy candles for light at night, and I worry that some crazy person might break in and hurt me or the kids, because there are no streetlights either,' she says.

During the six-month work season her family doesn't go hungry, but they only eat meat twice a week because a kilo costs 140 pesos (about $8). Eggs cost 60 pesos ($4) a carton, she says, 'so it takes half a day's work just to buy one.' She's paid by the hour, making 900 pesos a week, or 150/day ($9), for the normal 6-day week.

. . . There's no sewer service, and although there is a water line, the water is almost unusable. Since the mid-1970s big growers and their U.S. partners have pumped so much water from the desert aquifer that salt has infiltrated the groundwater.

High-tech

High-tech consumer electronics, such as laptops, iPhones and iPads, represent icons of contemporary global capitalism, as their globally dispersed production and sale integrates workers, firms and consumers across the world. In much mainstream GVC analysis, these industries are presented as generating potential win–win developmental outcomes. They embody the latest hard and soft technologies (machines and management techniques), are subject to rapid innovation, and generate high profits, and workers are described as receiving relatively high wages.

Apple stands at the pinnacle of the high-tech chain. It controls its supply chain tightly through outsourcing component production and assembly to different firms across the globe which must respond quickly to its evolving design innovations. It maintains its market dominance through high investments in product innovation, the use of patents to protect designs, and the employment of legal means (litigation) to enforce patents (Thompson 2012). Kraemer, Linden and Dedrick (2011) show how Apple's profit for the iPhone in 2010 constituted over 58 per cent of its final sale price, while the Chinese workers' share was 1.8 per cent (figure 3.1).

Apple also plays an important role in determining workers' very long hours. Its *Supplier Responsibility 2014 Progress Report* states

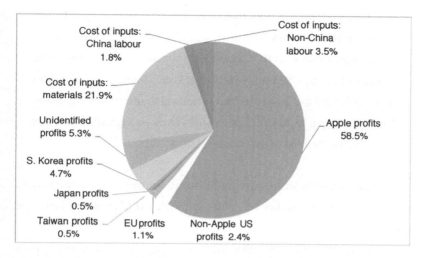

Figure 3.1 Distribution of value for the iPhone, 2010
Source: Kraemer et al. (2011: 5).

how the company requires its 'suppliers to achieve an average of 95 percent compliance with our maximum 60-hour week' (Apple Inc. 2014; Fuchs 2016). This is in stark contrast to the International Labour Organization's Convention C030 on work hours, which recommends upper limits of forty-eight hours per week and eight hours per day (and see below).[8]

There have been repeated media exposures of the poor conditions suffered by workers across the global high-tech sector. In Chinese computer assembly plants, 'workers are forbidden from talking during work, and are fined for not sitting properly. . . . [In one plant] managers have the right to fire workers who step on the grass in the factory complex. In another factory, workers who are caught littering must wear a placard saying "I am a garbage producer"' (CAFOD 2004: 33). In the early 2000s, for example, the Catholic Agency for Overseas Development (CAFOD) exposed the industry's practices of super-exploitation in Guadalajara, Mexico, detailing how:

Pay, although higher than that of workers in factories producing for the domestic market, is low: typically, US$50–US$100 a week at companies such as IBM. A worker must do excessive overtime to earn close to US$100. A basket of basic food, rent, transport and clothing for a family of four amounts to about five times the legal minimum wage, and electronics workers typically earn less than half of the cost of that basket. (Ibid.: 23)

Even if two parents were working full-time for these firms, they could not afford a basic basket of goods without working many hours of overtime.

In China's Pearl River Delta, low-cost labour employed by Apple's suppliers is guaranteed by a state-designed and -regulated labour regime. The *hukou* system of household registration segments the labour market by establishing a temporary migrant labour pool of rural workers who are classified as non-residential workers in urban areas, and who experience lower pay than and legally inferior rights and conditions to their urban counterparts. This 'floating population' comprises up to 70 and 80 per cent of workers in the manufacturing and construction sectors, respectively (Ngai and Chan 2012; Friedman 2014; Clelland 2014; Foster and McChesney 2012).

In 2010, Foxconn, one of Apple's principal Asian suppliers, employed around 500,000 workers in its factories in Shenzhen and Chengdu. It rose to infamy that year following reports of eighteen attempted suicides by workers, fourteen of which were fatal (Ngai and Chan 2012). Foxconn employs a military-style labour regime. At the start of the day, managers ask workers 'How are you?', and staff must reply 'Good! Very good! Very, very good!' After that they must work in silence, monitored by managers and with strict limits on toilet breaks. Pay is low, and overtime is often the only way that workers can earn enough to live on. Following the attempted and actual suicides, and a wave of strikes and protests, Foxconn raised wages by up to 25 per cent (SACOM 2010: 9).

After these events, rising criticism of Apple for its suppliers' treatment of workers, the discovery of child labour in its supply chain, and the firms' own expansionary objectives, the TNC contracted another supplier – Pegatron near Shanghai – claiming that the move would contribute to raising labour standards. The contracting of Pegatron saved Apple approximately US$61 million a year because it can supply cheaper components based upon even lower wages and worse conditions than Foxconn (China Labor Watch 2015).

Pegatron workers earn around 21 per cent less than their counterparts at Foxconn and have worse weekday and weekend overtime rates. In 2014, Pegatron employees worked on average sixty hours overtime a month, and over half of its workers put in over ninety hours overtime a month. 'Workers desire overtime because their base wages . . . cannot meet the local living standard' (China Labor Watch 2015).

In his study of the sources of its super-profits, Donald Clelland (2014) highlights other factors that enable Apple to benefit from ultra-low-cost inputs. The long-term reproduction costs of the migrant labour force are borne by their households, largely through unpaid women's work. Among their other survival strategies, workers purchase cheap goods, services and meals from the vast army of informal street vendors.

Apple also benefits from the externalisation of nature. An iPad requires 79 gallons of water, sufficient fossil-fuel-based electricity to generate 66 pounds of carbon dioxide, and 33 pounds of minerals. The first generation iPad 'generates 105 kilograms of greenhouse gas emissions' (Clelland 2014: 102). The Asian NGO Friends of Nature shows that Apple suppliers cause water and air pollution, heavy metal discharges, and chemical emissions, endangering lives of people living near the factories (ibid.: 102). Because pollution costs are lower in China, Apple and its suppliers are able to externalise more of the environmental costs of production than if these activities were performed in Northern economies.

Implications for Northern workers

The establishment of super-exploited labour forces across the global South is the bedrock upon which the global manufacturing system stands. The establishment of this labour force has exerted colossal downward pressures on workers' wages across much of the global North, in at least five ways.

First, the production of cheap goods across the global South and their export to the global North have lowered the costs of Northern wages and capital goods. Lowering the former reduces the costs of reproducing labour power (and can contribute to pushing wages down). Lowering the latter reduces the costs of capital investments (such as new machines and services) (Milberg 2008; Strange and Newton 2006; Nolan 2003).

Second, 'offshoring' contributes to the restructuring of labour markets in ways unfavourable to labour. In the US, between 1979 and 1999, 'after losing their job, sixty per cent of service workers reported taking a pay cut when becoming reemployed.' Further, 'Long periods of unemployment and large declines in income are likely to persist among those affected by offshoring. Of the dozen occupations projected by the U.S. Department of Labour to produce the most jobs in the nation by 2008, half of them pay poverty wages. These high-growth jobs include janitors, cashiers, and home health aides' (Whalen 2005: 37). Donald Trump's presidential victory was based, in part, upon appealing to those workers that he claimed had been 'abandoned' by US capital.

Third, a long-term process of labour repression in the North through the strategies of demobilising labour by states and firms has reduced workers' real incomes. According to the Washington-based Pew Research Center's report on US wages:

After adjusting for inflation, today's average hourly wage has just about the same purchasing power as it did in 1979, following a long slide in the 1980s and early 1990s and bumpy, inconsistent growth since then . . . In real terms the average wage peaked more than 40 years ago: The $4.03-an-hour rate recorded in January 1973 has the same purchasing power as $22.41 would today.[9]

Fourth, the threat of offshoring represents a sword of Damocles that firms and states across the global North hang above the heads of 'their' labouring classes as they seek to raise the rate of labour exploitation (which they call raising productivity). Jack Welch, the former CEO of General Electric, told his shareholders that 'we must remove that lower 10 per cent, and keep removing it every year – always raising the bar of performance' (cited in Upchurch 2014). This strategy has become known as 'performance management', 'forced ranking', and 'rank and yank', where managers classify workforces according to their productivity with the objective of removing the least productive ones. Up to 60 per cent of US firms employ such techniques.[10]

Fifth, and as a consequence of the previous dynamics, super-exploitation is becoming increasingly prevalent and politically acceptable across the global North. For example, in their study of the greater Leicester region of the UK's apparel manufacturing sector, Nik Hammer and his colleagues note how 'Employers often consider welfare benefits as a "wage component" and force workers to supplement wages below the [national minimum wage] with welfare benefits. These problems are endemic in the industry: reports consistently put the average wage at £3 per hour and state that this applies to 75–90% of jobs in the sector' (Hammer et al. 2015: 10).

Reversing these downward trends will require mass movements and struggles across the global North. But they will also depend on whether the vast pool of super-exploited workers in the global South expands or contracts. A reduction in global capital's super-exploitation of Southern workers will, simultaneously, represent a blow against its capacity to pit Northern and Southern workers against each other. Victories for labouring classes across the global South should be celebrated by Northern workers' organisations, as the fate of both are inextricably linked.

∖_Conclusions

The global business revolution has transformed the structures and dynamics of global production and trade. In the immediate post-Second World War period, world trade was structured around a classical division of labour – where Northern economies produced and exported manufactures and imported raw materials, while Southern economies produced and exported primaries and imported manufactures. Today production is globally integrated, and Southern countries are as industrialised as, if not more so than, Northern countries.

The anti-poverty consensus and mainstream global value chain analysis celebrate and promote further the integration of Southern country economies into the global manufacturing system as a means of alleviating poverty and stimulating local-level development. However, a common feature of the value chains at the heart of the global economy is that they rest upon a continually expanding, super-exploited labour force. 'Normal' wages are, effectively, poverty wages that do not support workers' social reproduction. In order to secure adequately their everyday needs, workers in these industries must either work many hours of overtime or rely upon subsidies (often in the form of free food grown by family members on local plots), or both. These workers' health suffers, but it is not incorporated into the APC's conception of poverty. The consequences for labouring classes the world over are severe. That is why it is better to relabel global value chains as global poverty chains.

4

Deepening Exploitation:
Capital-Centred Development

Introduction

This chapter discusses a range of development theories to high-light their capital-centred conception of the world. It discusses the Washington and Post-Washington Consensus, varieties of pro-poor growth, statist political economy and modernisation Marxism. Each of these, albeit in different ways, conceives of workers as objects of the development processes. This objectification justifies theoretically and politically the exploitation, oppression and subordination of labour to capital-centred development. Under these conditions, capitalism's immense dynamism and wealth-generating capacity systematically accrues to a small minority of the world's population.

The chapter is structured as follows. The next section highlights, in broad conceptual brushstrokes, the elite assumptions that underpin all varieties of capital-centred development theory (CCDT). Section 4.3 deconstructs CCDTs in more detail, illuminating their differences and commonalities.

Capital-centred development theory: elite subjects, subordinate objects

While development thinking aims to contribute to the uplifting of the world's poor, its core traditions are founded upon assumptions about 'the poor' that contribute to their (re)subjection to debilitating hierarchical social relations. This is because the development of 'the poor' is dependent upon elite guidance. The poor are required to subject themselves, or be subjected, to elite-led processes of capital-centred development.

The elite subject–subordinate object (ES–SO) conception of capital-centred development reproduces itself in at least four ways in development theory, policy and practice:

1 it identifies capital accumulation as the basis for the development of the poor;
2 it identifies elites (whether corporations, state planners, private-sector agencies or NGOs) as drivers of capital accumulation;
3 myriad actions, movements and struggles by the poor are disregarded (i.e., not considered developmental) and are often considered to be hindrances to development; and
4 as a consequence of point 3, elite repression and exploitation of the poor politically and economically is legitimised, especially when the latter contest elite-led development.

The ES–SO conception of development represents what Michael Cowen and Roger Shenton label a 'doctrine' because it rests upon 'the intent to develop through the exercise of trusteeship over society. Trusteeship is the intent which is expressed, by one source of agency, to develop the capacities of another' (1996: ix–x). In this ES–SO conception, subjects possess primary agency, while objects possess only secondary agency once they have been incorporated into elite-led development processes.[1] The disempowered condition of objects is unrelated to the empowered condition of subjects. Empowerment of objects does not require disempowerment of subjects. Once development has been 'achieved', subjects retain their empowered status vis-à-vis objects. Capital-centred development theory cannot conceive of development being a process whereby objects, through their own actions and through the transformation of social relations, displace subjects from their elite position.

One of the most influential advocacies of capital-centred development was W. W. Rostow's (1960) post-Second World War modernisation theory, produced at the high point of what Philip McMichael (2000) calls the 'development project'. It is one of the clearest statements of CCDT because it aims simultaneously to facilitate rapid capital accumulation while eliminating other possible routes to human development. Rostow's *The Stages of Economic Growth: A Non-Communist Manifesto* posited five stages of economic growth (traditional society; preconditions for take-off; take-off; drive to maturity; age of high mass consumption) through which all countries could pass, provided they followed the correct (non-socialist) policies. The key concern for the US state, identified by Rostow and others (e.g., Huntington 2006), was to ensure that 'modernisation' would occur in the countries of the South, so that they could be incorporated fully into global capitalism without succumbing to the dangers of workers' and peasants' revolution. As Rostow warned:

It is in such a setting of political and social confusion, before the take-off is achieved and consolidated politically and socially as well as economically, that the seizure of power by

Communist conspiracy is easiest; and it is in such a setting that a [pro-capitalist] *centralised dictatorship* may supply an essential technical precondition for take-off and a sustained drive to maturity. (Rostow 1960: 163, emphasis added)

In an important critique of elite conceptions of social change, the Brazilian socialist educationalist Paulo Freire described how dominant elites construct legitimacy myths. The latter are part and parcel of capital-centred development theory:

the myth that the oppressive order is a 'free society' . . . the myth of the charity and generosity of the elites . . . the myth that the dominant elites, 'recognizing their duties', promote the advancement of the people, so that the people, in a gesture of gratitude, should accept the words of the elites and be conformed to them . . . the myth of the industriousness of the oppressors and the laziness and dishonesty of the oppressed, as well as the myth of the natural inferiority of the latter and the superiority of the former. (Freire 1972: 109)

At the heart of capital-centred conceptions of development, albeit with various nuances, is a representation of the capitalist market as a developmentally progressive sphere of individual and social opportunity and economic dynamism.

While capitalist development is creative, it is also destructive. The destructive aspects of capitalist expansion and reproduction are what Cowen and Shenton label 'immanent' development, while the ES–SO doctrine represents 'intentional' development. Immanent development refers to the underlying process of capitalist expansion, in particular the establishment of capitalist social relations (or 'markets' in much development parlance). Aspects of immanent capitalist development include (often violent state-backed processes of) mass dispossession from the land, the creation of propertyless wage-labour forces, the despoliation of human populations, unplanned urbanisation and the creation of mega-slums, and environmental destruction. Capital-centred development theories obscure and externalise these destructive aspects of development from the benign image of (intentional) development that it offers to the poor. Rather than focus on these destructive aspects, CCDTs focus upon what Cowen and Shenton label the 'intentional' and more benign aspects of development, such as 'human capital formulation' (i.e., training workers once they have been established within a labour market).

Part of the practice of intentional development is the provision of social policies to ameliorate the effects of immanent development. These policies are delivered within an ES–SO conception of the world. They are framed ideologically as forms of benign assistance to the poor as a result of the latter's exclusion from, or inadequate integration into, the market. This framing enables proponents of immanent development to argue continually for greater elite-led 'inclusion' of the poor within expanding capitalist markets. The ideologically debilitating effect of such a portrayal of social change is simultaneously to reproduce elite power vis-à-vis a disempowered mass. As Gustavo Esteva (1992: 3) puts it, for the world's poor 'to think . . . of any kind of development – requires first the perception of themselves as underdeveloped.'

To be sure, development under capitalism does transform the situations of the poor. But it does so by de/reintegrating them from one set of hierarchical relations into another. As we shall see, an indication of this is the way in which labour is conceptualised within CCDT as an input into, or a 'factor' of, production.

Labour as an object of development

This section illustrates through textual analysis and deconstruction how capital-centred development theory conceives of human labour and workers as inputs into the development process. This starting point simultaneously justifies labour oppression and exploitation and delegitimates labouring-class attempts at collective self-amelioration (see table 4.1).

The Washington/Post-Washington Consensus

The Washington Consensus (WC) conception of development represents the late twentieth-century ideology of pure free-market capitalism. It was used from the 1980s onwards to justify structural adjustment programmes designed to integrate further indebted countries into networks of global capitalism. It derives from Adam Smith's understanding of gains from specialisation, David Ricardo's theory of comparative advantage, and the emphasis of marginalist economics upon 'perfect' markets. Each tenet contributes, from its own perspective and when combined within the WC, to generating 'higher productivity and labour utilisation' (OECD, cited in Cammack 2013: 3).

Ricardo's theory is based on a simple truth – that each country performs a range of activities better than it does others. From this truth arises the (much debated) policy prescription that countries should specialise in the mix of activities they do best, which will maximise effective resource use and output. Goods can then be traded on the world market in exchange for goods that a society wishes to consume. If this theory is adhered to on a world scale, then global resource use will be optimised and the maximum range of goods will be produced at lowest cost. Specialisation and trade ensure a harmony of interests

Table 4.1 Commonalities of capital-centred development theory

Development theory		Market aspects		
		Economic growth as basis for development	Sanctity of private property rights	Market 'inclusio as development
Washington Consensus		Yes	Yes	Yes
Post-Washington Consensus		Yes	Yes	Yes
Pro-poor growth	Neoliberal varieties	Yes	Yes	Yes
	Decent work version	Yes	Yes	Yes
Developmental State		Yes	Yes, but conditional upon economic performance	Yes
Modernisation Marxism		Yes	No – private property rights largely replaced by state property rights	Yes, albeit markets organised by states

between different national economic units. What benefits one country benefits another – and their respective populations.

The Washington Consensus also adheres to marginalist axioms about perfect markets, where rigidities or inflexibilities within the latter reduce welfare gains from market participation. The concept of market inflexibility was utilised by WC proponents to theorise and justify (deleterious) reforms to workers' conditions. Such reforms aimed to re-establish the 'role' of workers in development as holders of a factor of production (labour) that could be effectively employed by

	Role of state			Role of labour	
	Market - correcting	Aim to facilitate 'embedded' and productive links with business elites	Carrier of 'factor' of production	Use of 'voice' to influence elite-led policy	Devise development policy
ket- rting	Yes, but rarely	No	Yes	No	No
	Yes, often	Yes	Yes	No	No
	Yes	Yes	Yes	Sometimes	No
	Yes	Yes	Yes	Yes	Only as subordinate actor to state and business elites
	Yes, following initial market distortion	Yes	Yes	No	No
	N/A	Yes, following state's commencement of capital accumulation	Yes	Sometimes	No

firms. Eliminating labour market inflexibilities would, according to WC theory, generate virtuous circles of rising firm profits, greater employment and higher economic growth. Labour market inflexibilities were defined by Robert Solow as follows:

A labour market is inflexible if the level of unemployment–insurance benefits is too high or their duration is too long, or if there are too many restrictions on the freedom of employers to fire and to hire, or if the permissible hours of work are too tightly regulated, or if excessively generous compensation for overtime work is mandated, or if trade unions have too much power to protect incumbent workers against competition and to control the flow of work at the site of production, or perhaps if statutory health and safety regulations are too stringent. (Solow 1988: 1)

The concept of labour market inflexibility justifies workers' political and wage repression in order to restore greater flexibility to this market. Such actions are portrayed as being in workers' long-run interests. For example, Anne Kreuger (the World Bank's chief economist between 1982 and 1986, and a strong advocate of structural adjustment for indebted and poor countries) argued that, 'with a sufficiently low urban wage, a zero unemployment level is a feasible outcome' (Kreuger 2007: 10).

The WC and neoliberalism more generally have been conceptualised as a political–ideological–social battering ram to be used by states and firms to reduce organised labour's influence in politics and economics. Its objective has been to establish 'capitalism without a working class opposition' (Reed 2014: 67).

From the above perspective, ensuring labour market flexibility represents a base line for successful economic development. Moreover, it is held to contribute to increasing freedoms of individuals that comprise a national society. An unmistakable statement of this logic was made by Friedrich Hayek after General Pinochet's murderous 1973 coup against Chile's democratically elected president Salvador Allende: 'I have not been able to find a single person even in much-maligned Chile who did not agree that personal freedom was much greater under Pinochet than it had been under Allende' (Hayek 1978).[2] The logical basis of Hayek's position – that any form of workers' democracy undermines capitalist efficiency, and therefore the common good

of society – was stated with greater brutality than later neoliberal jus-
tifications for labour market restructuring. But its logical opposition to
any form of workers' influence over the process of capital accumulation became the core of neoliberal ideology as it gained institutional
support from the late 1970s onwards.

For example, in its 1993 report on the East Asian miracle, the World
Bank argued that part of the success of the high-performing Asian
economies was their ability to limit labour market distortions. These
economies 'have generally been less vulnerable than other developing-
economy governments to organized labour's demands to legislate a
minimum wage'. Further: 'Because wages or at least wage rate increases
have been downwardly flexible in response to changes in the demand
for labour, adjustment to macroeconomic shocks has generally been
quicker and less painful in East Asia than in other developing regions'
(World Bank 1993: 19).

From the early 1990s onwards, however, the Washington Consensus
became increasingly untenable, following the failure of structural
adjustment programmes to regenerate growth, the proliferation of
'IMF riots' and continued protests against the effects of neoliberal
policy, notable research from statist political economists demon-
strating the centrality of states in generating growth in East Asia (see
below), increasingly severe financial crises across the globe, and, more
broadly, a recognition throughout development thinking that removing market inflexibilities (or 'getting prices right') did not suffice to
guarantee development.

These critiques generated a shift in the World Bank's thinking and in
development theory more broadly. From being conceived as distorting
markets under the WC, states and institutions became, under the Post-
Washington Consensus (PWC), potential correctors of market failures.
The shift from WC to PWC did entail a soft critique of the market insofar

as it was theorised as suffering, under certain conditions, from failures. As Hoff and Stiglitz argued: 'in leaving out institutions, history, and distributional considerations, neoclassical economics leaves out the heart of development economics . . . market failures are pervasive, especially in developing countries' (Hoff and Stiglitz 2001: 390, 391).

However, the critique was soft because the PWC argued that, with the correct state or institutional support, market failures could be negated and the benefits of well-functioning markets, as proclaimed by proponents of the earlier WC, could be realised. As Stiglitz said in his 1998 WIDER lecture, which is often identified as representing the emergence of the PWC:

Making markets work requires . . . sound financial regulation, competition policy, and policies to facilitate the transfer of technology and to encourage transparency . . . the government should see itself as complementary to markets, undertaking those actions that make markets fulfil their functions better – as well as correcting market failures . . . free competitive markets and private property' . . . [are] 'essential to market economy'. (Stiglitz 1998: 1, 22, 18)

While in the WC the theory of labour market inflexibility was used to rationalise reductions in workers' wages, worsening their conditions and constraining their organisations, Stiglitz approached labour differently. His advocacy of 'democratic development', sympathy for protests against the IMF and the World Bank, and support for workers' right to unionise set him apart from the anti-labour orientation of the WC.

Stiglitz's contribution to the transformation of neoliberal ideology reflected a broader socioeconomic–political process. Following states' and corporations' restructuring of organised labour during the market-fundamentalist phase of neoliberalism, the reduction of trade union bargaining power and the latter's embracing of many market-orientated norms (often under the ideology of the 'Third Way'), the conditions were established for a period of neoliberal consolidation through 'social neoliberalism'. The latter variant was softer than the former because opposition to it was weaker. As Neil Davidson explains for the British case, which is applicable to the shift from WC to PWC:

> the first [phase of neoliberalism – the WC] involved a frontal onslaught on the labour movement and the dismantling of formerly embedded social democratic institutions ('roll-back'); the second [phase – the PWC] involved a more molecular process with the gradual commodification of . . . new areas of social life and the creation of new institutions specifically constructed on neoliberal principles ('roll-out'). (Davidson 2013: 25; see also Peck and Tickell 2002)[3]

The PWC is concerned more with worker training, human capital formation, and the need to foment political legitimacy to engender workers' commitment to capitalist expansion than with simple labour discipline.

However, workers are still conceived, principally, as bearers of a factor of production. Thus Stiglitz writes that 'in the short run large scale involuntary unemployment is clearly inefficient – in purely economic terms it represents idle resources that could be used more productively.' There is a need for workers to feel that they have a stake in the system, otherwise employers will be subject to unreasonable claims: 'if workers believe that they are not being fairly treated, they may impose inflationary wage and other demands.' In the worst-case scenario, 'social and economic costs translate into political and social turmoil' (Stiglitz 1998: 25, 29, 1).

Stiglitz's relative inclusion of labour in his development theory compared to the WC is limited. This is revealed in his inability conceptually to connect his preferred cases of development, in particular the East Asian economies, with their extreme labour repression and exploitation. Rather, he sidelines these aspects and highlights, instead, the ability of states to create, support and regulate markets. He praises China's leadership for 'engag[ing] in extensive deliberations and consultations' in their attempts to overcome problems ranging from environmental destruction to overinvestment.[4] His focus upon relations between states and markets lessens his ability to integrate a fuller analysis of capital–labour relations into his understanding of human development. His portrayal of East Asian states' treatment of labour is misleading. In his best-selling *Making Globalization Work*, he writes that 'East Asian nations feel that it is their responsibility to maintain full employment and actively promote growth, and their governments remain concerned about inequality and social stability' (Stiglitz 2007: 49). He does not mention how successive East Asian governments used violence to repress their labour movements and mould populations subservient to heightened exploitation (and see below).

In Stiglitz's hands, the PWC is beset by a dualism. On the one hand, it advocates fairer treatment of labour. On the other hand, its favoured cases of development, in particular in East Asia, are characterised by heightened labour repression and exploitation. Stiglitz overcomes this dualism by ignoring the latter cases of exploitation and oppression and by excluding these concerns from its conception of capitalist development. He can do so relatively easily because, across the range of capital-centred development theory, labour is conceptualised as primarily an input into the development process. It is therefore of second-order analytical importance compared with state policies to achieve well-functioning markets. Few capital-centred development advocates would therefore take Stiglitz to task for his simple conceptions of capital–labour relations.

Pro-poor growth and decent work

The PWC's partial transcendence of the WC's market fundamentalism (through its recognition of the necessity of non-market institutional support for markets) has contributed to the emergence of a range of approaches to economic growth that aim to benefit the poor, such as 'pro-poor' growth and 'decent work'. That economic growth needs to be thought of in 'pro-poor' or 'inclusive' terms reflects, however, an unspoken recognition that growth is often 'pro-rich' and 'anti-poor'. While the 'pro-poor' growth perspectives are relatively liberal, the 'decent work' concept is more social democratic. Advocates of these approaches range across the World Bank, the International Labour Organization (ILO) and most national governments.

A line of differentiation between these conceptions is the extent to which, and the ways in which, they are pro-poor. The more liberal approaches, advocated, for example, by the UK's Department for International Development (DFID) and Overseas Development Institute (ODI), and by the World Bank, propose an absolute conception of pro-poor growth, which is achieved when the poor's economic conditions are improving. The more social democratic approach, as advocated by the ILO, proposes a relative conception, where growth is pro-poor when poor people's incomes are rising faster than those of the better off (Saad-Filho 2010).

The above approaches can be interpreted as attempts to apply PWC principles to development policy. Like the PWC, they emphasise institutions, state support for the market, and measures to 'include' the poor and workers in economic growth. For example, in the ODI's absolute conception of pro-poor growth, the institutions that facilitate successful policies and economic outcomes include 'a stable macroeconomy; institutions that allocate property rights, lower transaction costs, and permit organised production in companies and collectives'. Poverty reduction requires providing physical access to markets, remedying market failures, investing in a population's education and health, and countering discrimination. The ODI favours (limited) wealth redistribution because it can contribute to economic growth and reduce inequality and vulnerability, which in turn enables risk-averse households to take advantage of investment opportunities. It objects to 'excessive' redistribution such as large-scale transfers from rich to poor, as they may 'reduce incentives to invest, innovate and . . . to work, thus dampening economic growth' (ODI 2008: 3).

The social democratic concept of decent work, as promoted by the ILO, focuses upon labour conditions as a determinant of economic growth and the extent to which workers can simultaneously contribute to growth and benefit from it. Decent work involves:

> opportunities for work that is productive and delivers a fair income, security in the workplace and social protection for families, better prospects for personal development and social integration, freedom for people to express their concerns, organize and participate in the decisions that affect their lives and equality of opportunity and treatment for all women and men.[5]

The ILO advocates a tripartite approach to securing decent work through a corporatist model of collaboration between state, business and trade unions. States play a central role in fomenting globally competitive business sectors in ways that bear more similarity to statist political economy's analysis of the successful East Asian economies than to the 'market correcting' agenda of the PWC. However, strong state intervention and support for business are couched in social democratic terms rather than in the dictatorial terms of some of the harder formulations of statist political economy (see below). The 'voice' of workers is part of the ILO's conception of a fair economy. It is to be articulated through legal trade unions and heard by employers and the state. In return for listening to and negotiating with workers, trade unions respect business profits and business's 'right' to organise the labour process. In a similar vein to the ILO, the ODI argues that:

> Giving the majority, and particular the poor, a stronger voice in policy-making promises to lead both to better policy-making as well as to demands on the state for accountability, with consequent pressure for more effective and efficient public services. . . . [F]ormal democracy and decentralisation can help, but may not be sufficient . . . Recent development success stories are notable for gains to the poor resulting from the initiatives of *enlightened elites*. (ODI 2008: 4, emphasis added)

Notably, both the ODI and the ILO cite contemporary China as achieving pro-poor growth (ODI 2008; ILO 2014). Like Stiglitz (above), neither explains the significance to its developmental trajectory of China's non-democratic political system or its exploitative and repressive labour regime. Neither do any of these institutions recognise the progressive impact of more than a decade of rising struggles by urban and rural workers on the Chinese state's more 'enlightened' labour policies (see also chapter 5).

Common to all these conceptions of pro-poor growth is the axiom of labour as a factor of production, where its use is to be determined by profit-orientated corporations. The ILO, ODI, DFID, World Bank and most national and global development agencies argue for 'win-win' development, where rising firm-level productivity, facilitated by state-implemented policies, generates increasingly rapid economic growth, rising social surpluses and rising wages. Accordingly, this virtuous circle not only pulls workers out of poverty but also enables them to participate increasingly in public and political life by articulating their 'voice'. Workers enjoy limited secondary agency (but never primary agency) in that, when they are organised into trade unions, they can push for greater transparency and enlightened policy from state bureaucrats and/or better employment standards from employers.

Statist political economy

Statist political economy (SPE) is rooted in the work of Alexander Hamilton, Friedrich List, and the post-Second World War emergence of development economics, encompassing thinkers such as Gerschenkron, Kaldor, Hirschman and others. Contemporary advocates of SPE, drawing on Chalmers Johnson's concept of the developmental state, include Robert Wade, Ha-Joon Chang, Alice Amsden, Atul Kohli and Peter Evans.[6]

SPE represents a partial critique of liberal, Ricardian economics. The notion of development based upon comparative advantage is criticised by SPE, which argues that contemporary developed countries did not industrialise according to comparative advantage maxims. Rather, they pursued 'infant-industry' strategies – including protective tariffs, subsidies and the provision of R&D to nascent industries, and reverse engineering. The promotion of comparative advantage maxims by already developed countries and Northern institutions such as the

World Bank is therefore portrayed (correctly) by SPE as hypocrisy (Amsden 1989; Wade 2004; H.-J. Chang 2002).

While many states attempted to facilitate rapid industrialisation through the above-mentioned strategies in the twenty to thirty years following the Second World War and decolonisation, many failed to do so. To explain these divergent outcomes, SPE emphasises the importance of state capacity, often achieved through the establishment of elite planning bodies. Peter Evans's concept of 'embedded autonomy', drawing on Max Weber's (1978) concerns with bureaucratic rationality, represents an attempt to theorise dynamic relations between developmental state bureaucracies and business elites that generate long-term economic growth and industrial transformation (Evans 1995).

Johnson's discussion of Japan's Ministry of International Trade and Industry (MITI) and Amsden's and Wade's analysis of South Korean and Taiwanese industrialisation, respectively, provide strong empirical support for the above theoretical claims (Johnson 1982; Amsden 1989; Wade 2004). SPE survived the neoliberal ideological counterrevolution (unlike other traditions, in particular the varieties of dependency, world systems and Marxian theories) and was arguably one of the schools that forced the World Bank to agree to the research which generated the eventual publication of its *East Asian Miracle* report (World Bank 1993). The latter represented a partial admission by the World Bank that East Asian economies did not industrialise rapidly because of their adherence to the doctrine of comparative advantage and limited state intervention.

Much of SPE's popularity within development thinking derives from its penetrating critique of the above-mentioned neoliberal axioms. However, it represents a case of capital-centred development theory par excellence, and often in a brutal form. In her study of South Korean industrialisation, Alice Amsden recognises that 'high profits in [its] mass-production industries have been derived not merely from investments in machinery and modern work methods . . . but also from the world's longest working week.' Alongside effective investments, 'cheap labour' and 'labour repression is the basis of late industrialization everywhere.' Amsden observes the impacts of the gender division of labour on women workers: 'The average wages of women workers . . . have lagged far behind those of men, enabling employers in the labour intensive industries to remain internationally competitive alongside the growth of a mass-production sector. Wage discrimination against women in Korea and Japan is the worst in the world' (1990: 13–14, 18, 30).

In his comparative study of late development in South Korea, India, Brazil and Nigeria, Atul Kohli illustrates the ability of the former state to allocate resources efficiently and successfully to implement long-term industrial upgrading strategies across the economy. He notes, like Amsden, the need for strict workplace discipline. He also compares South Korea to the interwar European fascist states and concludes that: 'Generally right-wing authoritarian . . . [these states] . . . prioritize rapid industrialization as a national goal, are staffed competently, work closely with industrialists, systematically discipline and repress labour, penetrate and control the rural society, and use economic nationalism as a tool of political mobilisation' (Kohli 2004: 381).

Dae-Oup Chang (2002), in his critique of SPE, documents how, in General Park's South Korea, trade unionists were sent to concentration camps. Contemporary China is often championed by statist political economists as formulating an alternative path to neoliberal capitalism. But, as in previous East Asian developmental states, labour repression and lack of democracy have been and remain core determinants of its ability to generate the world's biggest labouring class and subject it to intense discipline and exploitation (Breslin 2011; Gray 2014).

SPE, while representing a powerful critique of neoliberal comparative advantage theory, rests upon the same ES–SO conception of development. Both view workers as bearers of labour power, to be managed, disciplined and exploited in order to yield economic surpluses for further investment. In this respect, General Pinochet's neoliberal Chile and General Park's statist South Korea had much more in common than the intellectual rivalry between neoliberal theory and SPE might suggest.

None of the Asian success stories – Japan, South Korea, Taiwan and now China – even after long periods of rapid economic growth and industrial upgrading and diversification, can be said to have overcome the ES–SO relationship and the deleterious labour conditions that characterised their earlier (and in China's case ongoing) developmental efforts.[7] SPE rejects *a priori* the question of whether objects of development can self-transform into subjects of development, and whether this may generate novel and positive human developmental dynamics.

Modernisation Marxism

There are numerous traditions within Marxism, ranging from perspectives that dovetail with anarchist thought in rejecting capitalism and embracing revolutionary socialism from below to those that portray capitalism as a progressive socioeconomic force, and which advocate state-imposed socialism from above (Draper 1966). The latter perspective, which was never adhered to by Marx, became an almost religious doctrine in Russia following Stalin's assumption of total leadership of the USSR in 1928. From that time onwards, Soviet socialism would be achieved through state-implemented five-year plans designed to accelerate the country's industrialisation and enable it to compete militarily with the West.

Following the ₍USSR's emergence as the world's second superpower and the 1949 Chinese revolution, the five-year plan model of top-down industrialisation became popular across much of the Third World. Stalin's explanation of the need for rapid Russian industrialisation struck a chord with newly independent countries struggling to find their geopolitical and economic footing in the emerging US-dominated world economy: 'The pace must not be slackened!' he said in February 1931. 'On the contrary we must quicken it as much as is within our powers and possibilities . . . We are fifty or a hundred years behind the advanced countries. We must make good this lag in ten years. Either we do it or they crush us' (quoted in Deutscher 1967: 328).

The millions of deaths under Stalin and Mao, as a consequence of attempts at accelerated industrialisation, deterred neither state leaders in the Third World nor development theorists from adopting variations of modernisation Marxism to explain and facilitate state-led socialist development from above. Why did these 'socialist' forms of development generate such misery? An important body of literature demonstrates how the cases of 'really existing socialism' were actually forms of 'state capitalism' (see Cliff [1974] on Russia, Harman [1974] on Eastern Europe, Harris [1978] on China, Binns and Gonzalez [1980] on Cuba, and Zeilig [2010] on myriad sub-Saharan African cases). This literature identifies October 1917 as a genuine workers' revolution. It also notes how, following international isolation and intervention, famine, de-industrialisation and the physical disappearance of the pre-1917 industrial working class, it was defeated from within by Stalin's emerging state bureaucracy.

Following the model of Stalinist Russia, new post-colonial ruling classes used the state to accumulate capital rapidly, by means of exploiting of their countries' working classes and peasantries, in order to compete in and attempt catch-up with more economically advanced capitalist countries. The developmental 'successes' – in particular rapid industrialisation and militarisation – of 'really existing' socialist states certainly influenced academic conceptions of Marxism. Whether or not they subscribed to Stalinist development strategies, these variants of Marxism portrayed capitalism and capital accumulation as a dynamic and progressive force in human developmental terms.

Within development studies, modernisation Marxism was theorised and given renewed popularity in the 1970s. The title and substance of Bill Warren's *Imperialism: Pioneer of Capitalism* captures the positive dynamism ascribed to capitalism by him and his followers. For example, in John Sender and Sheila Smith's prognosis for sustained economic growth in Africa, the authors argue that 'rapid accumulation is unlikely to be achieved without significant reductions in the real incomes of a substantial proportion of the population.' To achieve such accumulation, African states must become viable political entities, entailing the containing of 'sub-nationalist pressures' through 'a combination of hegemonic official nationalism and the military means to reinforce this ideology . . . a method must be devised for the appropriation of sufficient surplus to ensure the smooth functioning of the military and repressive apparatus.' While Sender and Smith advocate 'placing the issues of trade-union rights, wages and working conditions on the political agenda', they argue that this is only possible 'within the context of serious attention to feasible economic strategies.' Such concerns, however, are always subordinate to the more pressing issue of achieving rapid capital accumulation. And the latter requires a repressive political economic apparatus (Sender and Smith 1986: 77, 112, 132).

Sender's later work on the prospects for African socioeconomic development, about which he is relatively optimistic, articulates an updated version of modernisation Marxism. It provides only a small space for workers' secondary agency: 'If capitalist accumulation in poor countries becomes more dynamic, it can create the potential for organized and successful opposition to its own excesses and irrationalities' (Sender 1999: 110).

In his reinterpretation of Marx for the global age, Meghnad Desai argues that the former would have been 'on the side of the market' and that a contemporary progressive political programme entails support for the expansion and full functioning of market forces, free from state interference. Following Marx, Desai recognises that the capital–labour relation is exploitative as it enables capitalists to capture unpaid labour from workers. However, he then argues that the relationship is good for workers, and that the latter should support such a relationship: 'If employability depends on high profitability, workers would want to cooperate with employers in keeping profits high . . . If workers know the rule "no profits, no employment" then they will struggle, not for a higher share of wages in total output, but with that share that maximises their chance of employment' (Desai 2002: 3, 65–6).

Gavin Kitching (2001) argues that capitalism is the most progressive force in human history and that many on the left misunderstand its potential to eliminate global poverty. Accordingly, the fastest route towards ameliorating the poor's condition is not through class struggles from below but by redesigning the rules governing the world economy in order to realise fully Ricardo's vision of a globally integrated system organised around the principles of comparative advantage.

Modernisation Marxism often uses socialist language to advocate rapid capital accumulation and integration into global product markets. However, it represents another variant of the ES–SO doctrine of development designed to generate a strong industrial economic base. In this way it has more in common with distinctly non-Marxist conceptions of development. For example, Atul Kohli, an advocate of statist political economy, observes the 'uncanny resemblance between how communist and cohesive-capitalist states [of which South Korea is the prime example] generate power resources to accomplish their respective goals' (Kohli 2004: 384). Philip McMichael highlights a core similarity between East and West during the development project: 'Although the two political blocs subscribed to opposing representations of human destiny, they shared the same modernist paradigm. *National industrialisation* would be the vehicle of development in each' (McMichael 2000: 30, original emphasis). Once labour is subordinated to capital, then the question of resource allocation becomes confined to the sphere of elite-dominated politics and economics.

Unsurprisingly, the fundamental unity in advocating labour subordination between (Post-)Washington Consensus, SPE and modernisation Marxism is not emphasised by these traditions. Doing so would limit their claims to exclusivity and might open the door to more critical approaches to human development.

4.4 Conclusions

Capital-centred development theory and practice, ranging across a wide political spectrum, sustains the reproduction of social relations that maintain the disempowered conditions of the world's poor. CCDT self-legitimates in at least three ways: through the identification of elites, ranging from state planners and policy-makers to capitalist corporations, as primary actors in the development process; by ignoring and delegitimising the poor's actions to uplift themselves, unless these actions complement elite conceptions of development; and by legitimating the exploitation and repression of the poor.

The ideological power of CCDTs is that, from within their frame of reference, they disable consideration of non-elite forms of human development. Moreover, their ideological support for labour repression means that, even when such alternatives arise, they are often put down. The essential paradox of CCDT and practice is that it advocates the oppression and exploitation of labouring classes for the ostensible benefit of those labouring classes. The next chapter, in opposition to CCDT, provides a theoretical basis and an empirical analysis of labour-led development.

Resisting Exploitation:
Labour-Led Development

Introduction

Against the capital-centred development theories discussed in the previous chapter, this chapter argues for an alternative development paradigm that allocates primary agency to labouring classes. This requires an enquiry into, an investigation of, and an attempt to theorise how collective actions by labouring classes can generate developmental improvements for themselves and their communities.

Following this introduction, section 5.2 provides the foundations of labour-led development (LLD) theory, and section 5.3 provides contemporary examples. These illustrate how collective labouring-class actions can generate both immediate material improvements in the livelihoods of the participants and their communities and novel organisational and collective resources.

A theory of labour-led development

Capital-centred development theory and practice views capital's needs (of accumulation, enhanced competitiveness and systematic appropriation of workers' unpaid labour) as the basis for achieving human development. It also views labour from the perspective of capital – where labour's needs (for better living and working conditions and higher wages) are achieved by securing, first, capital's needs. Capital-centred development theories view the world through the lens of capital and represent, in one form or another, the political economy of capital. But this is not the only form of political economy that derives from the analysis of capitalist class relations. These relations generate an alternative political economy – the political economy of labour – and, deriving from it, alternative understandings of and strategies for achieving human development.

In his inaugural address to the First International, Marx provided two examples of the political economy of labour. The first, the Ten-Hours Act (introduced in England in 1847), which legally reduced the working day to a maximum of ten hours, was the first time that 'in broad daylight the political economy of the [capitalist] class succumbed to the political economy of the working class.' The second example was the creation of worker-run cooperative factories. The latter were significant because 'By deed instead of by argument . . . [such organisations] . . . have shown that production on a large scale, and in accord with the behests of modern science, may be carried on without the existence of a class of masters employing a class of hands' (Marx 1864).

The political economy of labour views labour power from the vantage point of labour rather than from the vantage point of capital.[1] This generates a fundamentally different, and opposed, world view to that advanced by capital-centred development theories. As Michael Lebowitz describes: 'The value of labour-power looks different from the two sides of the capital/wage-labour relation. Just as for capital it is the cost of an input for the capitalist process of production, for workers it is the cost of inputs for their own process of production.'

Consequently: 'Two different moments of production, two different goals, two different perspectives on the value of labour-power; while for capital, the value of labour-power is a means of satisfying its goal of surplus value . . . for the wage-labourer, it is the means of satisfying the goal of self-development' (Lebowitz 2003: 127). The existence of two potentially rival political economies is constitutive of (i.e., it shapes) capitalist development in (at least) two ways. On the one hand, 'capital does not merely seek the realization of its own goal [accumulation]; it also must seek to suspend the realization of the goals of wage-labour' (ibid.: 122). This suspension is observable in CCDT's ideological legitimation and practical contribution to demobilising labouring classes and subjecting them to elite direction.

However, the potential existence of a rival political economy is constitutive of capitalist development in a second way. Workers' collective gains against capital are won through 'negating competition, . . . infringing on the "sacred" law of supply and demand and engaging in "planned co-operation"' (Lebowitz 2003: 84, citing Marx). Such collective actions and the elite responses to them, and the institutional formations that occur subsequently, often engender the more progressive features of intentional capitalist development, such as workers' rights, welfare provision, and various forms of democracy (see the following section on the capitalist state).

Capital-centred development theory views the relationship between labour and capital as follows:

$$K-WL-K',$$

where K = capital and WL = wage labour. In this schema, capital reproduces and expands itself (accumulates and heightens its competitiveness) through its employment/exploitation of wage labour in order to produce exchange values (goods to sell on the market) and production of surplus value (K') through the institutionalised capture of workers' unpaid labour. From the vantage point of capital, any disruption to its employment of wage labour harms not only capital's objectives of accumulation but also labour's objectives of higher wages and better living and working conditions. A range of strategies designed by capital to discipline labour are therefore theoretically and practically justified.

In 'productivist' variants of Marxism, the above schema (K–WL–K') is approached from the vantage point of the workplace with a sole focus upon surplus-value production and extraction and workers' resistance to it. But, as outlined in chapter 2 (and below), such interpretations are unduly limited. The reproduction of the circuit of capital implies and is co-dependent upon the reproduction of the circuit of wage labour. Struggles within the circuit and over the social reproduction of wage labour are as important to a labour-led development perspective as those within the sphere of production.

A labour-led development (LLD) perspective starts from the opposite side of the capital–wage labour relation, which it views as follows:

$$WL–K–WL.$$

Here workers must sell their labour power to capital in order to earn the wages required to sustain themselves. Capital mediates the reproduction of labouring-class needs – through determining whether or not workers are employed (and, if so, under what conditions). However, in this context of mediation, the objectives of labour are not simply and totally subsumed under those of capital. They are sought by workers *within* and sometimes *against* capital. Workers, whether employed or unemployed, whether engaged in productive or reproductive labour, can act collectively against capital's attempts to determine the form and extent of their social reproduction.

From the above perspective, the core concerns for LLD theory are not those of capital (how to enhance accumulation) but those of labouring classes. These may include provision of resources to secure and ease the social reproduction of labour (for example, the provision of child care, education, free or cheap food for children at school and beyond); gender and ethnic equality (to reduce differential rates of exploitation); the attainment of higher wages and better conditions in work; more free time through shorter working days and more decision-making ability within the workplace to reduce the burden of work; sufficient time and space to secure the basic necessities of life and to be able to get to and from work safely; access to the means of production (e.g., land, factories, workplaces) and survival (e.g., water and electricity); adequate housing and nutrition; and the ability to engage in culturally enhancing activities such as education, socialising and, most importantly, leisure.[2]

While CCDT claims to point to a future characterised by a high and rising level of human development, the way it views the capital–wage -labour relation (K–WL–K′) illustrates how, for labouring classes, that future will be one eternally circumscribed by the needs of capital. If capital is unable to realise its objectives of accumulation and enhanced competitiveness, labouring-class needs are expendable. LLD's view of the capital–wage labour relation (WL–K–WL), by contrast, suggests a variety of ways in which labouring classes can reproduce themselves vis-à-vis capital (including various forms of control/regulation of capital). It also opens the way to enquiring how, and under what circumstances, labouring classes can reproduce themselves and fulfil (identify, meet, expand) their human developmental needs beyond capitalist social relations.

States and the capital-labour relation

States play a central role in constructing and managing the political and legal structures within which capital accumulation and the social reproduction of class relations occur. These structures constrain, through law, workers' ability to organise themselves and engage in collective actions. Capitalist states work to naturalise and implement across society the norms, practices and social relations of the political economy of capital. States engage in building institutions designed to structure the behaviour of their citizens and social classes, simultaneously to reproduce state power and to guarantee the process of capital accumulation. 'Institutionalisation involves not only the conduct of agents and their conditions of action, but also the *very constitution* of agents, identities, interests and strategies' (Jessop 2001: 1230, emphasis added).

However, states also respond to labour's collective actions in ways that individual firms do not. The production and reproduction of state institutions 'is incomplete, provisional, and unstable, and . . . coevolve[s] with a range of other complex emergent phenomena' (Jessop 2001: 1230, 1228). State institutions, ranging from those established to manage the capital-labour relationship (such as ministries of labour), to provision of welfare, to their democratic forms, can themselves be understood as outcomes of evolving contested relations between capital and labour.

States can, in other words, incorporate and institutionalise (usually in order to neutralise) aspects of the political economy of labour to a degree that individual firms cannot. This means, however, that moments in state-capital-labour relations emerge in which labouring-class pressure for change is institutionalised in ways to its benefit (before being eroded by a counter-movement by capital). An important challenge for labouring-class organisations, then, is to retain and defend institutionalised gains, as well as to develop new strategies to extend and deepen them.

Labour-led development: contemporary examples

Mass struggles from below have been and continue to be drivers of world-historical change and human development (Seidman 1994; Silver and Arrighi 2001; Silver 2003; Selwyn: 2015c). These struggles range from the fight against Atlantic slavery and for better working conditions in European industries in the eighteenth and nineteenth centuries, to the European and American interwar strike-waves and revolutionary movements that pushed ruling classes to introduce welfare states, to the mass strikes during the 1980s against dictatorships in Brazil and South Korea and apartheid South Africa.

This section discusses how labouring-class collective actions can extract developmental gains from states and capital and generate new organisational forms that further enhance their and their communities' livelihoods. These collective actions range across and often combine attempts to improve conditions in productive and reproductive spheres. Cases discussed vary from formal to informal sector and across agriculture and industry (see table 5.1).

Shack dwellers' movements in South Africa: Abahlali baseMjondolo

Contemporary South Africa is characterised by extreme wealth and mass poverty. The ending of apartheid and the ascent to political

Table 5.1 Contemporary labour-led development – some examples

Countries	Example, sector, formality
South Africa	Shack dwellers' movements (informal), mineworkers and metalworkers (formal)
Argentina	Piqueteros, unemployed workers' movement, recuperated factory movement (informal to formal)
Brazil and India	Agrarian-based Movimento dos Trabalhadores Rurais Sem Terra, agricultural workers in Bihar (informal)
China and Indonesia	Industrial wage workers (formal)

power of the African National Congress (ANC) represented a moment of hope in South Africa and beyond. The 1996 constitution aimed to make meaningful universal citizenship and recognised the right of all South Africans to basic services and housing. Despite the ending of apartheid and the black economic empowerment initiative established by the ANC, poverty continues to be racialised.

Approximately 47 per cent of the population live under the national poverty line (US$43 per month in 2013), of whom over 90 per cent are black. The numbers living on under US$1 a day doubled between 1994 and 2006 – from approximately 2 to 4 million. The average rate of unemployment was 26 per cent in 2004, while for black South Africans the rate more than doubled between 1991 and 2002, from 23 to 48 per cent (Klein 2008: ch. 10). Between 1994 and the mid-2000s, around 2 million South Africans were evicted from their homes because of non-payment for services that they could not afford (Miraftab 2006).

In a context of limited job opportunities, mass poverty and inadequate state provision of basic human necessities, shack dwellers' movements have emerged across the country's shanty towns. Through collective actions they have pressured local government for resources to meet basic human necessities – in particular, housing and sanitation

– and they have self-generated 'human resources' to provide services to their members and wider shanty-town communities.

In 2001, an anti-eviction movement (AEM) coalesced in Cape Town. Its mobilising and campaigning strategies range from informal nego-tiations to mass protests, sit-ins and land invasions. The movement also possesses 'struggle plumbers and electricians' who reconnect the services of disconnected households and help relocate evicted families to their housing units. The AEM has won victories, including achieving municipal rate exemption for houses worth less than 50,000 rand and getting moratoriums on evictions and service cut-offs in many poor townships, and in some cases banning banks' eviction of the elderly and disabled (Miraftab 2006: 199, 198).

In the mid-2000s, another, even larger shack dwellers' move-ment emerged across the country. Founded in 2005, by 2013 Abahlali baseMjondolo (also known as AbM) had more than 12,000 members across more than sixty shack settlements. The movement emerged from the Kennedy road settlement in Durban, where, in 2005, 8,000 people shared only five drinking water standpipes. Abahlali combines mass street protests with land occupations to pressure local munici-palities and city councils to provide basic services. For example, in 2009, Durban city council agreed to provide drinking water, electrifica-tion and regularly cleaned latrines for fourteen settlements and formal housing for occupants of another three settlements (Birkinshaw 2008; Buccus 2009).

Abahlali operates through direct democracy – where, for example, negotiators with city councillors and leaders are directly electable and de-selectable and are subject to scrutiny in regular mass meet-ings (Selmeczi 2012; Gibson 2011). The movement's high level of participation has also generated new human resources – members vol-unteering to provide services to others and the wider shack settlement communities. These include provision of crèches, monthly food parcels cooked and delivered to the destitute, care for child-headed households and people with AIDS, and security and fire patrols at night (Pithouse 2006). S'bu Zikode, one of Abahlali's founder members, describes how:

> we cannot wait in the mud, shit and fire of shack life for ever. Voting did not work for us. The political parties did not work for us. Civil society did not work for us. No political party, civil society organisation or trade union is inviting us into the cities or into what remains of democracy in South Africa. We have no choice but to take our own place in the cities and in the political life of the country. (Zikode 2013)

Fighting for a living wage: South Africa's mineworkers and metalworkers

On 16 August 2012, thirty-four platinum miners at the Marikana mine were massacred by members of the South African Police Service (SAPS). The massacre was a response by the SAPS and owners of the region's platinum mines to increasing levels of workers' militancy. South Africa possesses over 85 per cent of the world's known platinum reserves. Historically, profitability in the industry was based upon regulating platinum supply onto the world market and keeping extraction costs down through an intensely exploitative labour regime (Capps 2015). Peter Alexander and his colleagues describe working conditions:

> Poverty ... at Lonmin, and fear of losing their jobs means [workers] tolerate some of the most arduous and dangerous conditions imaginable ... underground workers ... perform

heavy manual work, often doubled up, under the threat of rock falls and machinery accidents . . . the air underground is . . . full of dust and chemicals. TB is widespread and illness is common. (Alexander et al. 2013: 25)

The massacre exposed the ANC government as complicit with the mine-owners. The mineworkers maintained their strike, however, won a substantial pay rise, and, in so doing, contributed to an increase in militancy across much of the rest of the country. As Patrick Bond (2012) notes, 'The 22 percent raise – at a time inflation is around 6 per cent – they won after a month of striking was remarkable, and inspired the country's labour force to look at their own pay packets askance.'

In the years following the massacre, the number and intensity of mass strikes increased across South Africa. In early 2014, strikes by workers at the three main platinum producers demanded a 'living wage' that would increase wages well above their R5,000 a month. Their resilience, often in the face of hunger, won them a pay rise to R8,000 across the sector and contributed to yet further strikes elsewhere in the economy. Only a week after the settlement of the platinum strikes, metal workers organised in the radical National Union of Metalworkers of South Africa (NUMSA) walked out, also demanding a significant pay rise. As Immanuel Ness (2016: 175) documents:

In its third week, the strike against metals and engineering con-tractors forced Toyota, General Motors and Ford assembly plants in South Africa to suspend production. The strike was settled a month later when the metal sector agreed to a settlement that would raise wages for the lowest-paid entry-level workers by 10 per cent per year over the three years of the contract.

Rural struggles in Brazil and India

The Landless Labourers' Movement (Movimento dos Trabalhadores Rurais Sem Terra/MST) represents a significant case of LLD in Brazil. Between its foundation in 1984 and the mid-2000s the MST's membership grew to over 1 million. It is composed of former small farmers and rural wage labourers and their families who are unable to get access to land and of unemployed workers from urban areas seeking a rural livelihood. The organisation contests the highly unequal land structure in Brazil, where by 2008 around 3 per cent of the population owned over 60 per cent of all arable land (Zobel 2009).

The MST has pursued a long-term strategy of occupying and cultivating unused land and claiming land rights from the state. By the mid-2000s it had gained land-titles for more than 350,000 families. While it faces repression from the Brazilian state, it has also been able to work with state agencies to further its cause. The movement has, since its foundation, had political allies in the National Institute of Colonisation and Agrarian Reform (Instituto Nacional de Colonização e Reforma Agrária – INCRA), the federal agency responsible for land reform and registration (Wolford 2010; Vergara-Camus 2014).

The MST uses agrarian legislation to justify taking over 'unproductive' land. The Brazilian national constitution of 1988 (article 184) ruled that privately owned land must both be productive and fulfil social functions. The latter are met when workers are employed legally (e.g., not under conditions of slave labour) and when the environment is preserved adequately. While these definitions were formulated in intentionally vague terms, in the context of the transition from dictatorship to democracy at the end of the 1980s they have nevertheless provided the MST with ideological sustenance. Land occupation serves a double purpose of pressuring the Brazilian state to begin negotiations over its appropriation and redistribution and to establish the material and ideological basis for MST settlement communities. Settlements seek to produce their own food and to sell surpluses, often under brand names, onto local markets (Branford and Rocha 2002).

The movement rejects a market-based conception of land simply as a commodity to produce other commodities. As Wendy Wolford (2005) describes, its form of land use derives from a conception of human–natural relations that emphasises work, community and God. The movement is influenced by liberation theology and Paulo Freire's theory of the pedagogy of the oppressed. Individuals within the movement take on a range of socio-political responsibilities according to the principle 'Here we are all leaders' (Lucas 2001).

The MST aims to transform Brazilian agriculture from its current agro-industrial model to a more family-farmer-centred form. Key demands include producing food for local and national consumption rather than export, introducing agro-ecology through eliminating agro-toxins, and job creation in the countryside. As João Pedro Stédile, one of the movement's founder members, argues, the MST's struggle for land reform entails the 'democratisation of land ownership, access to education at all levels and the development and application of new agricultural techniques' (Stédile 2004: 39; and see the following chapter). As one MST member and participant in land occupations in the early 1990s explained: 'Land conquered through the struggle has to be everyone's. It should not be for an individual. Land should not be a commodity so people can divide it and sell it. Land is meant to produce. One has to use it. If one doesn't, then one should pass it on to someone that will work it' (quoted in Vergara-Camus 2014: 183).

While the MST has faced repression from the Brazilian state and hostility from the media, it has demonstrated its ability to organise collectively and to generate human developmental gains. On the settlements 'people know that their fate is in their hands' (Stédile 2004: 39). The MST has, in turn, influenced other unemployed workers' movements in Brazil. In parallel and often in cooperation with the MST, an urban movement has emerged seeking to ameliorate the livelihoods of its members and their communities. Between 1997 and 2005, homeless workers' organisations in São Paulo mobilised approximately 10,000 people to occupy and live in empty buildings. The best known of these organisations is the Movimento dos Trabalhadores Sem Teto (Homeless Workers' Movement – MTST). The MTST follows in the footsteps of the favela movement, which resisted shanty-town evictions during the 1970s. In the urban sphere it works in collaboration with other social movements such as the União Nacional de Moradia Popular (National Low-Income Housing Union).

Just as the MST organises its members to occupy land, the MTST organises unemployed and informal-sector workers in urban areas to occupy and live in vacant buildings, hence establishing the basic essentials of a livelihood. In the early 2000s the MTST also began establishing, in collaboration with the MST, 'rurban' (rural-urban) settlements on the peripheries of cities on which its participants could combine agricultural activities (rearing animals and planting crops) with the search for city-based work (Levy 2011; Souza 2007).

Mass rural struggles are also an ever-present feature of Indian society. Over the last thirty years or so, women agricultural labourers in Bihar, eastern India, have fought for land redistribution, an end to caste discrimination, and a living wage (Wilson 1999, 2008). In this region, women workers have borne the brunt of highly concentrated land and class and caste power. Sexual harassment and rape by landlords of *dalit* women (considered by upper castes as 'beyond' or 'below' the traditional caste system) was, for a long time, considered normal behaviour deriving from caste superiority/privilege.

But women workers have managed to change the dynamics of caste and class power. Kalpana Wilson describes how:

> Women labourers have played a central role in wage struggles, . . . initially [placing] wage demands before employers, and subsequently collectively refus[ing] to work. Women have also led marches of thousands to physically occupy land for redistribution . . . It is women who, armed with bricks, small scythes or household utensils, have driven the police out of their villages when they have arrived heavily armed in midnight or dawn raids, or who have surrounded police jeeps and snatched back those arrested, even forcing the police to apologise in some instances. (Wilson 2008: 87–8)

Consequences of these long-term struggles are that women workers are now able to challenge these forms of oppression. Landowners have also been forced to recognise the dignity of agricultural labourers. As one such worker explained: 'Before if I remained sitting on the khatia outside my house when a landowner walked through this tola, he would abuse me or even beat me up. Now after we have got organised, I can carry on sitting here and invite him to sit down' (cited in Wilson 1999: 317).

From informal to formal sector: the Piqueteros, unemployed workers' and recovered factory movements

Since the 1990s, Argentina has witnessed multiple economic crises but also the rise of myriad interconnected forms of LLD. Between 1991 and 1995, the national unemployment rate increased from 6 to 18 per cent, partly caused by falling competitiveness due to an appreciating peso

(Dinerstein 2010: 358). Following the 1997 East Asian crisis and the 1998 Brazilian devaluation, Argentinian economic competitiveness vis-à-vis Brazil fell further and the cost of international loans increased (following rising interest rates in Europe and North America). Despite cutting wages and shedding jobs, Argentinian firms could not regain competitiveness. These dynamics were magnified by the crisis at the turn of the century. By 2001, up to 40 per cent of the population were living under the national poverty line. The extent of the economic catastrophe was comparable to the one that affected the United States and Germany between the wars (Harman 2002a).

Under circumstances of impoverishment and fast-retreating state welfare provision, increasing numbers of the population began to engage in diverse and interconnected forms of collective action, which, in some cases, coalesced to generate notable bottom-up developmental dynamics.

The Piquetero movement emerged in the mid-1990s as an organisation of unemployed workers which sought to wrest concessions from the state through blocking roads and disrupting the circulation of goods through the economy. From the mid- to late 1990s there were tens of such roadblocks a year throughout the country, rising to hundreds in the crisis year of 2001. The Piqueteros attempted to unite local communities and unemployed workers to demand from the state job creation, public works to provide essential services, and their participation in the management of employment programmes previously run by the central state (Dinerstein 2010: 358). In 2001 Piquetero collective actions escalated, with over 100,000 people shutting down more than 300 motorways and effectively paralysing the economy. These actions pressured the Argentinian state to provide thousands of minimum-wage temporary jobs and food allowances to local communities (Petras 2002: 2).

The Piquetero movement generated new forms of collective agency and autonomy vis-à-vis the state. Their actions were orientated simultaneously upwards (towards the state) and outwards (through their communities). In the late 1990s the Unemployed Workers' Movement (UWM – Movimento de Trabalhadores Desocupado) emerged from the Piqueteros and continued the earlier strategy of blocking roads, but it also began pressuring the state for more resources and for the political autonomy to manage those resources across their communities. The UWM's community projects include maintaining and repairing schools, hospitals and other public buildings, the construction and running of community soup kitchens, recycling rubbish, organising volunteers in retirement homes, providing healthcare and visits to the disabled, establishing small-scale craft production, offering childcare and milk in schools, establishing bakeries, providing basic education and health promotion, and improving sanitation (Dinerstein 2015). State-funded temporary jobs are distributed by the UWM through collective decision-making and are based on considerations such as families' needs and their members' participation in the UWM (Petras 2002).

One of the regions where the UWM have had their biggest impact is the town of General Mosconi in the Salta region of North-West Argentina. By the early 2000s the movement had generated hundreds of community projects to provide food for the unemployed both within and beyond the UWM. These included organic gardens, bakeries, first-aid clinics, and water-purifying plants. The extent of the UWM's coordination of the local economy meant that the town was 'ruled de facto by the local unemployed committee, as the local municipal offices have been pushed aside'. Furthermore, 'The emergence of a "parallel economy", on a limited scale, in General Mosconi sustains popular support between struggles and offers a vision of the capabilities of the unemployed to take command of their lives, neighborhoods, and livelihoods' (Petras 2002: 4, 5).

A third form of LLD emerged in Argentina in the late 1990s, expanded rapidly in the early 2000s, and has been maintained to the present. The recuperated factory (*fábricas recuperadas*) movement responded to the threat of rising mass unemployment by taking over and running factories that had gone bankrupt or been shut by their owners under conditions of worsening economic crisis. By the mid-2000s, approximately 15,000 workers had taken over and were self-managing around 200 enterprises across the country, ranging from metallurgical companies, food- and meat-processing plants, and printing companies to hotels and supermarkets and health and educational services (Atzeni and Ghigliani 2007). The example of the Brukman factory is indicative:

> We were going on fifteen days during which, although there was a ton of work, they didn't pay us a cent. There was growing unrest that broke out on the fifth floor, in the pants section, where there was a smaller group than ours . . . Their anger was boiling over faster than ours, and they practically stopped production . . . Supposedly we took home a hundred pesos every Friday, but that was already history at this point. (Matilde Adorno, Brukman worker, cited in Lavaca Collective 2004: 67–9)

The movement collaborated with the Piqueteros and the UWM in coordinating workplace production with community projects. By 2005 the movement controlled most of the factories in the country's southern province of Neuquén (Meyer and Chaves 2009: 167). In 85 per cent of cases of expropriated factories, national, provincial or municipal subsidies have helped support *fábricas recuperadas* and, furthermore, 82 per cent of occupied factories have received financial support from other *fábricas recuperadas*. The latter prevents an over-reliance on state subsidy, helping these factories remain relatively independent, worker-controlled spaces (Fishwick and Selwyn 2016: 240).

While the *fábricas recuperadas* are defensive in that they have maintained workers' employment, in some cases they have also been able both to expand the numbers of jobs in the factories under their control and to raise productivity. For example, the occupied Zanón tile factory (in Neuquén) underwent a notable transformation under workers' control:

> In October 2001, the workers officially declared the factory to be 'under workers' control'. By March 2002, the factory fully returned to production. During the period of workers' control, the number of employees has increased from 300 to 470 . . . wages have risen by 100 pesos a month, and the level of production has increased. Accidents have fallen by 90%. (Elliot 2006)

Tile production grew from 1.07 to 4.31 million square feet per annum between 2005 and 2008 (Meyer and Chaves 2009: 171). In occupied factories an alternative work ethic emerged: 'Workers defend their own power over the organization of production and the decision-making process by proudly stressing their freedom from direct/supervisory control, the existence of egalitarian relations and the benefits of democratic participation' (Atzeni and Ghigliani 2007: 659). In these cases hierarchical power structures have been replaced, or at least modified, by assemblies where workers meet to discuss and decide questions of factory management and by management councils which are elected by the assemblies to take charge of daily administration, commercial responsibilities and legal representation. New jobs created in Zanón were initially allocated to members of the UWM in the region. Meyer and Chaves (2009: 174) describe how:

What they [Zanón] do not invest in production, they allocate toward public works serving the needs of the people. From the beginning the Zanón workers donated tiles to first-aid facilities in one of the poorest barrios of Nequén, as well as to schools and even for the reconstruction of a hospital in Santa Fe . . . they also promoted, together with unemployed workers, a program of public works under the slogan 'jobs for all.' They make monthly donations to soup kitchens and hospitals.

Mass strikes in East Asia

From the 1990s onwards China has been characterised by an intense and highly exploitative labour regime where workers' living standards have been squeezed to ensure rising profits for capital. Consumption as a percentage of Chinese GDP fell from 44 per cent to under 39 per cent between 2002 and 2010 (Foster and McChesney 2012).

The number of mass protests across China has risen over the last two decades – from 10,000 incidents involving 730,000 protesters in 1993 to 60,000 incidents involving more than 3 million protesters in 2003 (Silver and Zhang 2009: 176). In 2009 there were more than 90,000 mass incidents across the country (China Labour Bulletin 2012). These struggles drove wages up by 17 per cent between 2009 and 2010. These struggles have had a cumulative impact, trebling Chinese industrial wages between 2005 and 2016.[3] Such mass protests have pushed the Chinese government to make concessions to labour:

Between 2003 and 2005, the central government and the Chinese Communist Party began to move away from a single-minded emphasis on attracting foreign capital and fostering economic growth at all costs to promoting the idea of a 'new development model' aimed at reducing inequalities among classes and regions as part of the pursuit of a 'harmonious society' . . . Likewise . . . the [state-run] All-China Federation of Trade Unions amended its constitution to 'make the protection of workers' rights a priority' in 2003. (Chan and Kwan 2003, cited in Silver and Zhang 2009)

Strikes, in which female workers are increasingly prominent, are an expanding form of 'mass incident': there were 1,171 strikes and protests in China between mid-2011 and the end of 2013, around 40 per cent of which were in manufacturing industries concentrated in the Pearl River Delta. Women workers are an increasingly large section of the labour force in and beyond industry (China Labour Bulletin 2014).

The composition of the industrial workforce has changed, with a second generation of migrant workers increasingly prominent. Their relative permanence in the urban/industrial sector has contributed to more militant confrontations with managers rather than to the practice, as with first-generation migrants, of abandoning jobs and searching for new ones (Ness 2016: 139).

One of the most recent high-profile 'mass incidents' was the strike at the Dongguan factory of Yue Yuen, the world's largest athletic shoe manufacturer. The strike, which stopped production for eleven days in April 2014, was one of the biggest such actions at a private enterprise in China. It occurred in response to revelations that the company had underpaid social security payments for the workers' medical insurance, injury compensation, housing allowance and pensions. The strike's intensity pushed the Chinese Ministry of Human Resources to force Yue Yuen to repay its workers.

Indonesia represents another zone of mass labour militancy.[4] The country has experienced rapid immiserating growth since its embrace of the neoliberal principles of openness, deregulation and low wages from the late 1990s onwards. Rapidly expanding palm oil and manufacturing sectors have generated large labouring classes that subsist on poverty wages. Workers' struggles have pushed up the minimum wage. Over a million workers struck across the country in October 2012, and more than 500,000 workers took to the streets to celebrate May Day in 2013. Their actions increased the minimum wage by 20 per cent between 2011 and 2012 and by 44 per cent between 2012 and 2013, raising the minimum wage to a level that local government considered adequate for meeting 'decent living needs' (Hauf 2016: 139).

External barriers to labour-led development: class and state power, market forces and political incorporation

Gains by labour can be neutralised or reversed through counter-movements by organised capital and capital-friendly sections of the state. Capital's ability to respond to labouring-class demands through new strategies of exploitation and accumulation can undermine labouring-class movements. The power of the capitalist market, manifested in never-ending competitive capital accumulation, exerts a reactionary pressure upon organisations that seek to engender alternative, non- (or at least lower) profit-orientated modes of resource generation and distribution. And the organisational political immaturity of labouring-class movements makes them susceptible to political capture and influence by more established and institutionally integrated conservative political forces. These four pressures represent external barriers to the extension of LLD.

For all their dynamism, the cases of LLD discussed in this chapter have been vulnerable to such pressures. Segments of the Piquetero movement have been co-opted into supporting electorally the left wing of the established Peronist political organisation, thus blunting their escalatory potential (Dinerstein 2010). Some of the *fábricas recuperadas* preside over rising worker self-exploitation (increased working hours and an intensification of the labour process) (Atzeni and Ghigliani 2007). The upward curve of land occupations and struggles that characterised the MST during the 1980s and 1990s came unstuck following the Workers' Party (PT) electoral victory in 2002. Part of the PT's strategy to establish its power within a hostile political environment was to incorporate its supporters into the Brazilian state through employment within the country's vast civil service and political system. A consequence of this was the declining independence of pro-PT organisations. MST land invasions fell from 285 in 2003 to thirty in 2011 and thirteen in 2012 (Vergara-Camus 2014: 305, n.7). Despite its objective of maintaining political independence, in 2014 Abahlali baseMjondolo supported the centrist Democratic Alliance (Brown 2014).

As argued in section 5.2, the reproduction of the political economy of capital is predicated upon the denial and undermining of the political economy of labour and the movements and collective actions that nourish it. The identification of the above-mentioned external constraints suggests the need for dialectical labour-led responses. This can occur through the formulation of novel organisational strategies and designs, as well as an identification of, and attempts to generate, counter-socio-institutional forces that can protect and advance labouring-class gains. Analysis of what such organisations and institutions have looked like, and speculation as to what they might look like, would contribute to the extension of LLD theory and practice.

Conclusions

Labour-led development ameliorates the conditions of its protagonists and their communities. These struggles and movements establish new forms of democratic practice and new ways of generating, distributing and conceiving of material resources. LLD has the capacity to shift systems of production, distribution and exchange away from domination by profit-orientated exchange values and towards socially necessary production. These cases and others potentially represent embryonic elements of a future, non-exploitative and cooperative society. The final chapter suggests the kinds of strategies and policies that could bring about such a society.

6

Beyond Exploitation:
Democratic Development

In the near future a labouring-class movement (comprising formal- and informal-sector wage labourers and the unemployed and their families), supported by a small-scale farmer sector conquers political and economic power in a relatively poor country through a combination of parliamentary elections and extra-parliamentary mass movements. The following is a draft discussion chapter prepared on behalf of one of the emergent political parties within the nascent state. It is designed to contribute to debates about the kinds of developmental strategies, practices and policies that such a movement and state could undertake.

Introduction

Capitalist development is predicated upon the exploitation of labour, the appropriation of wealth (ranging from women's unpaid labour, to environmental 'free gifts', to capital) and the categorical creation and oppression of 'second-class' citizens. Democracy under capitalism is of the 'low-intensity' variety – where decisions over economic resource generation and use are off-limits to the majority of the population, and where political systems facilitate the (mis)representation of the electorate (Gills and Rocamora 1992; Chomsky 1991). Capitalist development enhances the privilege and wealth of a tiny minority of the world's population and underpins the prevalence of global labouring-class poverty.

The following represents a radically different developmental agenda. It advances a vision of development which can be thought of as a minimum utopia – 'a form of society which could generally provide for its members the material and social bases of a . . . contented existence . . . from which the gravest social and political evils familiar to us have been removed' (Geras 2000: 44). The achievement of this minimum utopia will, in turn, generate further forms of human development.

This agenda is predicated upon the establishment of participatory economics and radical democracy. Unlike popular theories of participation (see Hickey and Mohan 2004), it is founded upon the capturing, holding and transformation of state power. It rejects, therefore, arguments for 'changing the world without taking power' (Holloway 2002). Given the power of capital, it is politically naïve to expect expanding (socially, politically-economically and geographically) labour-led development to occur without collisions with capitalist states.

The rest of this chapter is organised as follows. Section 6.2 discusses the possibilities and difficulties of a transitional phase of labour-led development. Section 6.3 outlines ways in which a labouring class state can be reconfigured and restructured *through* society. Section 6.4 argues that radical redistribution of wealth, in the context of changing social relations, represents the most rapid route towards realising a minimum utopia. Section 6.5 presents a ten-point plan for democratic development. Section 6.6 concludes the chapter and the book.

Contested reproduction and intermittent revolution

The initial conquest of political power will not mean the transcendence of capitalism but will represent a new, heightened phase of that struggle. It will be undertaken using tools inherited from the past: 'It must be kept in mind that the new forces of production and relations of production do not develop out of nothing, nor drop from the sky, nor from the womb of the self-positing Idea; but from within an antithesis to the existing development of production and the inherited, traditional relations of property' (Marx [1939] 1993: 278). There will be numerous firms where capital–labour relations still exist. Large numbers of unemployed workers will be seeking work and incomes. Households will still, in all probability, be led by women, dependent upon work-based incomes, and orientated towards (re)producing current and future generations of workers. The majority of land will probably be held by a small minority of capitalist farmers and/or landowners. Foreign trade will occur on capitalist terms. Financial institutions and their power within the economy will remain highly concentrated. Gender, racial and ethnic discriminations will continue to exist. Democratic institutions will be dysfunctional from the perspective of establishing a genuinely participatory society.

Under such circumstances, the policies and strategies of an emergent democratic state need simultaneously to expand and to enhance the dynamism of labour-led development while reducing the power of capital. Such a situation represents a transitional phase – where the old capitalist system is dismantled while a new democratic system is constructed. It will be crisis-prone. Michael Lebowitz describes this condition as one of contested reproduction: 'because there is contested reproduction between different sets of productive relations, the interaction of the systems can generate crises, inefficiencies, and irrationality that wouldn't be found in either system in its purity. . . . Two systems and two logics do not simply exist side by side. They interact. They interpenetrate. And they deform each other' (Lebowitz 2015: 96–7, 192). This point emphasises the progressive historical process of constructing an alternative society. Much time will be required to subordinate capitalist social relations to democratic social relations.

In the twentieth century the 1917 Russian Revolution was the single case of a workers' conquest of nation-state political power. The leaders of the revolution, Lenin and Trotsky, argued (correctly) against their political opponents that, even though it was economically 'backward', Russia was ripe for a socialist revolution because of the existence of a politically powerful working class. They also argued (correctly) that socialism in Russia could not exist in isolation and that, for it to survive and thrive, socialist revolutions elsewhere in the world, and in particular in more 'advanced' capitalist countries, would have to emerge and come to its assistance.

The initial gains of the Russian Revolution were world-historical (the first of their kind): Russia withdrew from the world war; extensive land-reform transferred the property of lords to peasants; workers gained control over production; the oppressed nations of Russia were granted freedom through self-determination; only civil marriages were recognised; children born out of wedlock were granted the same rights as those born in marriage; divorce was granted to either spouse for the asking; and homosexuality and adultery were dropped from the criminal code (Cliff 1987). The ideals of the French Revolution, of liberty, equality and fraternity, were realised briefly.

Lenin and Trotsky also assumed, or at least hoped, that international revolution (what Trotsky called permanent revolution) was on the cards. But it was not. The rise of Stalin through an effective domestic counter-revolution, and his commencement of state-capitalist development in 1928 under the banner of 'socialism in one country', spelled the end of the revolutionary experiment.

Why this digression? Because it is erroneous to expect the conquest of political power by labouring class in one country to be the catalyst for an *instantaneous* wave of 'permanent revolutions' across other countries. It is doubly necessary, therefore, to consider how an emerging labouring-class state can maintain the initial enthusiasm and energy of the classes that have created it, facilitate their enhanced social reproduction, and contribute, *at an unknown time in the future*, to the global expansion of democratic human development.

The process of enhancing labouring-class power will occur over the short, medium and long term, and will take many forms, including the construction of alternative institutions (cooperatives and communes); alternative means of securing and expanding the means of survival (the production and distribution of food and other basic necessities); new systems of participatory education; and the medium- and longer-term accumulation of political experience (of defending and extending the gains of labouring-class power). An outward-looking foreign policy can complement the domestic extension of labouring-class power through collaborating with international social movements to construct solidarity for the new regime (and, crucially, to defend it from hostile intervention) and, when opportunities arise, to extend labouring-class power internationally (see below). Such a process may be called intermittent revolution (Tugal 2016).

The initial emergence and establishment of a democratic labouring-class state in one country is the precondition for the emergence of other such states. And the advent of the latter is necessary in order to preserve the gains of the former over the long run. In all likelihood there will be a significant time lag between the emergence of the first such state and its global multiplication. It is within this time lag that a democratic development strategy must be formulated and pursued.

Reabsorption of the state by society

After studying the Paris Commune, Marx argued that it was 'the political form at last discovered under which to work out the economical emancipation of labour', as it would 'serve as a lever for uprooting the economical foundations upon which rests the existence of classes, and therefore of class rule' (Marx [1871] 1966). He characterised the radical process of changing social relations, and in particular of the relation of state to society, as 'the reabsorption of the state power by society as its own living forces instead of as forces controlling and subduing it, by the popular masses themselves, forming their own force instead of the organised force of their suppression – the political form of their social emancipation' (ibid.).

Societal reabsorption of the state is required to subordinate and transform capitalist social relations. Chapter 5 illustrated how labour-led development generates new forms of cooperation and democratic planning. These forms can be extended, deepened and qualitatively transformed in the process of transcending capitalism, as represented by the following three organisational principles:[1]

1 *Social ownership of the means of production*: As illustrated in chapter 3, capitalist 'commodity production has been the social form under which the most completely developed system of social interdependence in human history has been achieved' (Barker: 1998, 3). However, the means of production are directed autocratically, in accordance with market imperatives of competitive

capital accumulation. Such ownership structures deprive workers of any say over how and to what ends production is orientated and reduce them to 'objects' to be manipulated by managerial 'subjects'. Social ownership of the means of production, by contrast, would reconstitute decision-making as a collective democratic process.

2 *Labour-led social production*: The *social ownership* of the means of production facilitates the *social direction* of production through worker–community cooperation. Such cooperation is an essential property of an emergent democratic society for two reasons. First, because it limits, reduces and eventually eliminates production based upon autocratic and anarchic competition. Second, because the lifeblood of democratic development is cooperation (within and beyond workplaces).

3 *The identification and satisfaction of communal needs and purposes*: Under capitalism, rival firms vie to secure competitive advantage. Labouring-class households and individual members compete against each other to secure the best jobs. Communally based organisation within and beyond workplaces represents an alternative logic of social reproduction. The identification and satisfaction of communal needs and purposes will be predicated upon cooperation within and between workplaces and communities. This will also, potentially, contribute to the transformation of families – by relieving their basis in unpaid women's labour (see below).

How might these organisational principles be put into practice? A process of decentralised, local-level participatory planning represents one possible method (Harnecker 2014; Lebowitz 2015). Under such a system, the social energy generated by planning (drawing up and enacting a plan) flows upwards – from the local to the national level – rather than only downwards from firms and states, as under capitalism. A principle informing such a process is that 'everything that can be done at the lower level should be decentralised to this level' (Harnecker 2014). The national economy will be reorganised towards achieving these objectives. Needs and objectives that cannot be met at the local level will be transmitted upwards, to higher planning bodies, which can be incorporated into more general resource generation and allocation strategies.

The establishment and transmission upwards of democratic planning impulses require appropriate scales of participatory planning. These different but interdependent scales can be constituted by neighbourhood communities, communes, city/municipality councils and national state bodies.

Within a *neighbourhood community*, neighbours can meet regularly to discuss with each other what kind of community they want to live in and then identify and coordinate the community's needs and the abilities to fulfil those needs. The likelihood of a precise match between community needs and ability to fulfil those needs is small. The purpose of local-level planning is in part, therefore, to identify and to communicate upwards what additional resources are required and what surplus capacities are available.

The commune, which combines various neighbourhoods and workplaces, represents the next scale of decentralised participatory planning. Information from the communities is assembled and discussed within workplaces. Can workers satisfy the needs of the communities which comprise the commune? Under capitalism, where production is orientated towards the generation of exchange values (for profitable sale onto markets), such considerations are secondary (if present at all) to those of profit maximisation. Under an emergent democratic society, the identification of and attempts to meet local needs begin the process of substituting use values (goods produced to satisfy labouring-class needs) for exchange values. Through communal meetings, councils can generate data on:

(a) needs that can be and are satisfied by and within the community and commune,

(b) needs that cannot be satisfied by the community (which need further assistance from the commune and beyond),

(c) the surplus capacity in workplaces (which can contribute to meeting the needs of other communities and communes).

Surplus capacity and unmet needs are communicated further up the participatory planning chain to larger-scale units – from *communal cities* to the *national state*. As communes draw up their lists of needs, their (in)ability to meet those needs and their surplus capacities, the national-level state commune can assess how to generate and allocate resources. Where there are a great many needs, discussions will revolve around mechanisms to increase output, the (regional or social) real-location of resources, and/or possibilities for reducing the satisfaction of some needs.

Through decentralised participatory planning, participants attain knowledge about resource availability, production and allocation. In her distillation of the experiences of decentralised participatory planning in Brazil, Venezuela and India, Marta Harnecker (2014) writes how it represents a double process:

first . . . the plan, which has been elaborated in a participatory manner; and . . . second . . . the transformation of people through their practice . . .

[It] is an educational process in which those that participate learn to inquire about the causes of things, to respect the opinion of others, to understand that the problems they face are not exclusive to their street or neighbourhood but are related to the overall situation of the economy, the national social situation, and even the international situation. . . . Through this, new relations of solidarity and complementarity are created that place the emphasis on the collective rather than the individual.

Decentralised participatory planning will require some central coordination. Its extent cannot be determined in the abstract and would depend on considerations ranging from variations in different communes' abilities to meet their needs to changing global circumstances. In cases where communes are able easily to meet their own needs, it is probable that a relatively low level of central coordination would be required. In situations where there are stark regional communal disparities, a relatively higher degree of central coordination would be needed to coordinate resource transfers from more to less advantaged regions.

Redistribution: reclaiming social wealth

The core arguments of the anti-poverty consensus, and also their mainstream opponents, are that either capitalist economic growth is the fastest way to secure poverty alleviation and development (the APC) or that it provides at least the foundations for meaningful social progress (the APCC). The core argument in this chapter is that redistribution of wealth through the transformation of social relations represents the fastest means to alleviate poverty and, in so doing, establishes genuinely progressive possibilities and processes of human development.

It is often objected that, while such redistribution would contribute to meaningful human development in countries that are already wealthy (where the pie to be redistributed is relatively large), it is unlikely to do so in relatively poor countries (Ravallion 2009). These countries, rather, need to accumulate wealth prior to redistributing it, and, consequently, they must undergo a process of rapid capitalist development. Democratic development is thus precluded for one or many generations.

Such arguments often take for granted, or simply ignore, ways in which capitalist classes in poor countries are able to accumulate wealth, often offshore, and shield it from national taxation and potentially democratically determined use. For example, a study by Ndikumana and Boyce (2011) shows how:

> sub-Saharan Africa experienced an exodus of more than $700 billion in capital flight since 1970. . . . Africa is a net creditor to the rest of the world in the sense that its foreign assets exceed its foreign liabilities. But there is a key difference between the two: the assets are in the hands of private Africans, while the liabilities are public, owed by the African people at large through their governments.

This is compared to Africa's $177 billion in external debts (ibid.). The tax justice network in 2012 provided data for 139 'mostly low-middle income countries' and noted that:

> [T]raditional data shows aggregate external debts of US$4.1 trillion at the end of 2010. But take their foreign reserves and unrecorded offshore private wealth into account, and the picture

reverses: they had aggregate net debts of *minus US$10.1–13.1 trillion* . . . [T]hese countries are big net creditors, not debtors. [However], their assets are held by a few wealthy individuals, while their debts are shouldered by their ordinary people through their governments.[2]

Deborah Rogers and Bálint Balázs (2016) demonstrate that, in very poor countries, a relatively small distribution of wealth from rich to poor could eliminate poverty: 'Using numbers which approximate those of Bangladesh in 1995/96, a redistribution of 3 per cent of the income from the top quintile (reduced from 40.2 to 37.2 per cent) to the bottom quintile (raised from 9.3 to 12.3 per cent) results in a reduction in extreme poverty from 20 to 0 per cent.' They contrast this to the APC's preferred method of poverty reduction – economic growth: 'Attempting to reduce poverty by a similar amount through growth of the economy requires an expansion of total income of approximately 45 per cent' (ibid.: 62).

In a similar vein, Chris Hoy and Andy Sumner show how very limited wealth redistribution (through, for example, redirection of fuel subsidies away from their relatively well-off beneficiaries to the poor) can have significant effects: 'most developing countries have the financial capacity to end poverty at the . . . $1.90, or a slightly higher line of $2.50 and potentially $5 a day' (Hoy and Sumner 2016: 3).

In these calculations, rather conservative definitions of poverty are used. If more multidimensional conceptions of poverty were used, including poverty lines set at around a living wage level, then more income distribution would be required to eliminate poverty. Moreover, the above calculations presume limited wealth (money and income) redistribution within still existing capitalist social structures.

Our conception of democratic development considers all forms of wealth. Under capitalism, this wealth is socially produced but privately owned. Our objectives are to enhance the social production of that wealth *through* socialising its ownership and its democratic direction.

A ten-point plan for democratic development

This section proposes a ten-point plan for democratic development. Many of these proposals, in the absence of broader social transformation, are compatible with capitalism, and some of them have been implemented already. If these policies are compatible with contemporary capitalist development, then why and how would they contribute to constructing an alternative society based upon democratic development?

Whether a policy contributes to capitalist or socialist expansion depends upon the social relations within which it occurs and the objectives which it serves. For example, some socialists and some neoliberals support the idea of a universal basic income. The former support it (at a relatively high level) because it is understood as a contribution to reducing the market-based compulsion to work (mostly for low wages, under bad conditions and with no democratic input to the work process). The latter support it (at a relatively low level) because they see it as demolishing complicated welfare bureaucracies while maintaining the market-based compulsion to work (so-called incentives).

Policies can help engender democratic development if they contribute to the radical transformation of social relations. Progressive policies in the absence of social transformation will leave capitalist power intact, ready and able to undermine labouring-class gains. The ten points that follow derive, for the most part, from real-world experiences. They correspond, therefore, to a 'minimum utopia' agenda, where contemporary social life is improved and transformed using today's tools and resources. These will, if they are successful, establish the basis for further social transformations.

1 *Banks, money and economic democracy*

Money and private banks do not represent natural means and institutions for financial intermediation. On the contrary, they contribute directly to capitalism's growth dynamic, to class and regional differentiation, and to the concentration of capitalist power. Money and banks are social resources that can be held publicly or privately. They can serve either democratic or autocratic needs. The global financial system is not simply a mechanism through which money is allocated efficiently. Rather, it is a system of power which guarantees continued flows of global resources towards the dollar–Wall Street regime (Gowan 1999; Varoufakis 2011).

Our first objective will be to cancel what we consider to be odious debts (debts incurred by the previous administration for the benefits of capitalist rather than labouring classes). Following the lessons of the Greek economic crisis of 2015 (where a radical government attempted to negotiate debt reduction with the international 'community'), we will unilaterally write off debts (Flassbeck and Lapavitsas 2015).

We will introduce capital controls. Such controls, determined and implemented by a labouring-class state, will regulate the movement of capital in and out of the country and are the precondition for establishing democratic developmental processes (Marois 2012; Crotty and Epstein 1996). Such controls will regulate the export of money and finance (to prevent capital flight and to subject domestic capital to democratic imperatives). They will also serve to guide foreign investment towards socially dynamic and beneficial ventures, potentially in collaboration with local firms. As capital's exit options (which it uses to extract concessions from labour) are closed down, domestically generated resources which are still held in private hands will be invested domestically, under increasingly democratically determined conditions.

Under capitalism, banks effectively create money through loans (so-called sight money) (Mellor 2005). These accounts require growth to repay interest (which is typically lower for those who already have accumulated large stocks of money and higher for those without money). Central banks and states enforce the power of private banks by regulating the money supply to ensure that workers can obtain money only through selling their labour power, through (interest-based) loans, or through very limited welfare provision.

Under capitalism, scarcity is a consequence of class relations – of workers' lack of control over social wealth or the means of producing that wealth. A democratic society can begin to eliminate this scarcity by socialising finance – by integrating it into emergent cooperative structures, and by gradually replacing money derived from wages with a universal basic income (Mason 2016; and below).

Money will be increasingly conceptualised and function as a public resource and an instrument of democratic development (Mellor 2012). A new accounting system – encompassing local- and national-level associations – will calculate (a) the population's basic and extended needs (ranging from food consumption to infrastructure development requirements) and (b) the nation's available resources. Money will be distributed through state bank accounts to individuals and associations, in order to match society's resources (from raw materials to labour) with its democratically determined requirements/needs.

Rather than the state relying upon taxation to raise and invest money, money will be invested according to calculations of democratically determined need and resource availability. Where too much money is distributed (potentially leading to inflation) public taxation will be used to reduce the money supply. Remaining commercial banks will be transformed into intermediaries (between depositors and borrowers) and their operating costs will be met by user fees.

2 *A universal basic income*

Capitalist exploitation occurs because labouring classes lack the resources (such as money and land) to sustain themselves and are compelled to sell their labour power. A universal basic income (UBI) can contribute to eliminating this compulsion, to the construction of a solidarity-based political economy, and to the socialisation of much reproductive labour. It will also, immediately, alleviate many forms of deprivation and poverty.

Cash transfers in poor countries have helped combat poverty. For example, in the 2000s in Malawi, cash transfer programmes helped raise school attendance among girls by 40 per cent, and in Namibia they cut malnutrition (from 42 per cent to 10 per cent) and truancy (from 40 per cent to almost zero per cent) (Hanlon et al. 2012).

UBIs are affordable even for states with initially limited budgets and large poor populations. Cutting or eliminating subsidies to firms that do not produce for the (democratically determined) social good and those to better-off sections of the population can fund such grants initially.[3] The UBI will have one condition attached to it. Every able-bodied adult recipient will have a duty to carry out some unpaid household work within their community to support and care for those who are unable to take care of themselves. Only those who already do so will be exempt from the condition. Existing wealth and resources will, through redistribution, generate the increasingly free public provision of caring activities (such as nurseries, old people's homes, communal dining facilities and basic health facilities). The

UBI will complement such caring arrangements and will contribute to the restructuring of gender relations by socially recognising and distributing this work among the male population and by reducing the amount of women's domestic reproductive work (Elson 1988).

3 Industrial policy for a green transformation

The social ownership and direction of industry will contribute to establishing democratic development. The radical socialist National Union of Metalworkers of South Africa (NUMSA) argues that the most effective way to democratise the South African economy is through nationalising the highly lucrative mining sector. It draws on the 1955 Freedom Charter:

> The people shall share in the country's wealth! The national wealth of our country, the heritage of South Africans, shall be restored to the people; the mineral wealth beneath the soil, the banks and monopoly industry shall be transferred to the ownership of the people as a whole; all other industry and trade shall be controlled to assist the wellbeing of the people; all people shall have equal rights to trade where they choose, to manufacture and to enter all trades, crafts and professions.[4]

A democratic industrial policy aims to *shift* manufacturing away from exchange value (for profit) towards the production of use values (to serve the needs of workers and of the wider community). The shift will be managed to maintain some foreign exchange earnings to purchase essential industrial inputs and other goods. Export-orientated industries will be run by workers' councils, integrated into decentralised planning organisations. As shown in chapter 5 (in the cases of the occupied factories in Argentina) such factories can be expected to raise productivity and begin to diversify production.

Our industrial policy will seek to generate an appropriate mix of high- and low-tech activities orientated towards the satisfaction of basic (and extended) needs. Large-scale investments will be orientated towards generating a national green-energy generation system – comprising a mix of small-scale solar technology and larger-scale wind turbines connected to a national grid.

Relatively low-tech industrial research and development and expansion will focus upon areas such as the production and widespread distribution of stove heaters (such as rocket stoves), ceramic water purifiers, solar-powered desalination devices, toilet systems, lighting (e.g., gravity-powered lights), solar-heated showers, solar-powered lightbulbs, pot-in-pot refrigeration systems, and bike-powered water-pumps. Higher-end technological shifts will include transforming auto-plants into factories producing bicycles, buses and trains, beauty products into health-orientated pharmaceuticals, advertising into popular education, and arms into domestic appliances.

Intersectoral articulation – between industry and agriculture – will raise productivity in agriculture and establish a dynamic, innovative industrial sub-sector. Agricultural-industrial producer forums will be established to identify challenges and ways of meeting them – for example, through yield-enhancing investments in bio-technology.

The state will invest in establishing small-scale workshops in local communities. Such investments will make possible the expansion of neighbourhood economies based upon combinations of appropriate and high technologies. Where possible these workshops will be fitted with 3D printers. Such workshops would enable local-level production of many things that were previously accessible only through purchase.

They would also serve as recycling centres and locations for exchange of surpluses and information (see also Trainer 1996).

State investments in R&D will facilitate technology and knowledge transfer. These will be enabled and encouraged by non-market forms of exchange, such as open-access and peer-to-peer relations (contemporary examples include Wikipedia and copyleft and various forms of open-source software).

4 Agrarian reform

The global concentration of land is a product of imperialism, capitalist market imperatives and state support for land-based capital (Weis 2007; Akram-Lodhi 2015). This concentration and the prevailing export-orientated agro-industrial 'model' of agriculture denies workers access to the land and underpins the existence and expansion of a surplus unemployed population. It is also a causal factor in the 'paradox' of scarcity (lack of food for large segments of the world's poor) within abundance (global overproduction) (McMichael 1994).

The objectives of agrarian reform are (a) to contribute to the achievement of national food security (where enough food is produced to satisfy the populations' needs) and (b) to generate high-quality employment. In contrast to earlier examples of pro-capitalist agrarian reform, our objectives serve the goal of de-commodifying land, food and natural resources and, in so doing, establishing a society where adequate food consumption becomes a real human right. Such objectives do exist within a system of constraints. In particular, export agriculture often generates foreign exchange for necessary imports that cannot yet be produced domestically. Like our industrial strategy, our proposals for agrarian reform are based, therefore, upon a conception of a mixed agrarian system. Immediate reforms will include the transformation of ownership of large export-orientated estates – from capitalist owners to workers' cooperatives. These cooperatives will, in conjunction with national objectives, combine export production for foreign exchange with nationally orientated production for consumption.

The small-scale family farming sector will be preserved, but land would cease to be a (vendible) commodity. The universal basic income (see above) would provide social security for workers and family farmers (at times when they cannot produce). Common lands would be preserved and expanded.

The objective of achieving de-commodified food security, where food is a basic human right independent of purchasing power, will be sought through multi-level (from local communities to national state) investments to enhance sustainable, low-input agricultural productivity and through low- and high-tech R&D. Low-tech R&D includes facilitating building and conserving soil fertility, using biological controls for diseases, insects and weeds, intercropping, seed saving and selection, smaller-scale multiple harvesting cycles, and the integration of small-scale pasturing and grazing (Weis 2010: 334; Holt-Giménez 2002). High-tech R&D includes raising productivity through developing new plant varieties. As Kloppenburg (2010: 379) suggests, 'Participatory plant breeding offers a modality through which the labour power of millions of farmers can be synergistically combined with the skills of a much smaller set of plant breeders.'

Agrarian reform would extend into urban centres. Unused buildings can be transformed into greenhouses, flat roofs can be used as new growing spaces, unnecessary roads can be transformed into fields, allotments and parks, and home gardening will be encouraged and facilitated through provision of inputs, technologies and permaculture education. As Ted Trainer puts it, 'Most of this urban space can . . . be developed into permaculture forest-gardens, densely packed with mostly perennial plants so that settlements have permanent self-maintaining sources of food and many inputs for small craft producers' (Trainer 1996: 139).

5 Protecting and learning from indigenous peoples

From the 'discovery' of America in 1492 to contemporary globalisation, land grabbing, the dispossession of indigenous peoples, and the despoliation of natural environments have underpinned capitalism's geographical expansion (Clark and Foster 2009). Indigenous peoples have, however, often been at the forefront of opposing capitalist expansion and depredation and attempting alternative ways to live in conjunction with the natural environment. Joan Martinez-Alier (2003) refers to these struggles as the environmentalism of the poor. While preserving their land and cultural rights, an emergent democratic state will also establish forums to share knowledge and practice between communities. The protection and preservation of indigenous peoples' right to live according to their practices can potentially inform our conception of democratic development.

In parts of Latin America, the discourse and practice of *kawsay sumak* or *buen vivir* (living well) represents an alternative, potentially anti-capitalist conception of human development. It advocates 'living in plenitude, knowing how to live in harmony with cycles of mother Earth, of the cosmos, of life and of history, and in balance with every form of existence in the state of permanent respect' (Huanacuni 2010: 32; Carballo 2016: 183). The World People's Conference on Climate Change in Cochabamba, Bolivia, in 2010 represents a potential basis for our intended collaborative forum:

> Humanity confronts a great dilemma: to continue on the path of capitalism, depredation, and death, or to choose the path of harmony with nature and respect for life.

It is imperative that we forge a new system that restores harmony with nature and among human beings. And in order for there to be balance with nature, there must first be equity among human beings. We propose to the peoples of the world the recovery, revalorization, and strengthening of the knowledge, wisdom, and ancestral practices of Indigenous Peoples, which are affirmed in the thought and practices of 'Living Well,' recognizing Mother Earth as a living being with which we have an indivisible, interdependent, complementary and spiritual relationship.[5]

6 *Foreign policy (politics)*

Our foreign policy will be founded upon a dual approach. On the one hand, our guiding principle of external relations is non-aggression and the search for peaceful coexistence with capitalist powers. On the other hand, we will establish links with social movements around the globe that strive to transform their societies. Our assistance to these movements will consist of the demonstration effect. Information and practical knowledge about our short-term successes will be disseminated, and we will assist social movements to interpret them in the context of our longer-term social-transformative objectives.

We will seek to participate in international debates about alternative development strategies, to promote our experience and to explain its possibility and the extent of its applicability elsewhere. Our objectives will be (a) to strengthen transformative social movements to help them achieve their objectives, (b) to generate labouring-class pressures upon progressive capitalist states (i.e., states 'governed' by progressive parties) to provide us with development assistance, and (c) to facilitate similar pressures from below to preclude interventions by hostile capitalist states designed to undermine our transformative agenda. We will raise and promote the cause for a global living wage. We will form political alliances with movements, organisations and institutions that support this objective as a means of maintaining pressure for this and related policies and as a means of generating collaborative global networks.

We hope that, in the medium to long term, other states will undergo a complementary process of social transformation. We will strive to integrate these states into a global social commonwealth and to construct and transfer knowledge and resources between progressive states.

7 Foreign policy (economics)

As part of our economic foreign policy we will demand that the international community generate a collective agenda to combat environmental destruction. Our perspective will be adopted, in the first instance, from the Climate Justice Now (CJN) movement (which was established as a counter-movement to the rich-world-dominated Kyoto Protocol and global environmental agenda of carbon-trading, designed to legitimate continued fossil-fuel-based industrial expansion). The CJN proposes the following, which we believe can contribute to a genuinely progressive global development:

- leaving fossil fuels in the ground and investing instead in appropriate energy efficiency and safe, clean and community-led renewable energy;
- radically reducing wasteful consumption, first and foremost in the North, but also by Southern elites;
- huge financial transfers from North to South, based on the repayment of climate debts and subject to democratic control; the costs of adaptation and mitigation should be paid for by redirecting military budgets, innovative taxes and debt cancellation;

- rights-based resource conservation that enforces indigenous land rights and promotes peoples' sovereignty over energy, forests, land and water.[6]

Our foreign economic policy will be based on the concept of a transitional period of democratic development in a sea of autocratic capitalism. We will, therefore, seek to continue to engage in trade in order to raise foreign exchange to fund the purchase of necessary imports. As noted in point 1 above, capital controls will facilitate a progressive as opposed to a competitive integration into the world economy.

We will seek to attract development finance from progressive sources. We will approach trade unions, progressive municipalities and states (i.e., those led and governed by left-wing forces) and seek to persuade them to invest funds (such as their pension funds) in activities that will further our transformative agenda.[7]

Once other states and regions begin to undertake progressive social transformation, we will endeavour to generate close cooperative relations with them. Such relations will be determined by the human developmental needs and capacities of this emerging international collectivity:[8]

- *foreign trade and investment* will be directed by domestic democratic bodies (as noted above);
- *special and different treatment*: nations with greater developmental needs and lesser capacities will be granted preferential forms of access to the markets of nations that have greater developmental capacities;
- *cooperation and solidarity as development cooperation*: the collective struggle to raise populations' literacy and quality of health;

- *establishment of a social emergency fund* to assist emergent progressive nations to transcend (the inevitable) transitional crises of contested reproduction;
- *use of collective capacities* to enhance our global negotiating positions in areas affecting our future development, including trade and investment rules and environmental and labour standards.

8 Sharing and reducing work

Capitalism is founded upon a fundamental paradox. Technological advances have created a situation where only a tiny fraction of most societies' labour is required to fulfil its (basic and advanced) needs. However, private property, the drive to competitive capital accumulation, and labour's exploitation by capital disable this potential. Proposals 1 to 8 are designed to transform labouring-class control over work through (a) switching control over the means of production to labouring-class organisations and (b) altering the content and meaning of work through radical democratisation.

Initial objectives are to establish full employment for those that can work through the spreading and sharing of tasks. Longer-term objectives are to use democratic control over and social direction of the means of production to reduce the working day. Through the identification of needs of individual communities and of the nation as a whole, it will become increasingly possible to identify wasteful and/ or unnecessary activities and phase them out. Identification of necessary/socially desirable activities will contribute to the direction of our industrial policy. Research and development will be used to establish ways of increasing the efficiency and productivity of socially necessary/desirable activities with the objective of reducing the total working time required to create them.

9 *For gender equality and against nationalism and racism*

Attempts to generate democratic development will fail unless gender, ethnic and racial discrimination are overcome. In our endeavours to transcend these inequities we are inspired by the attempts of Kurdish independence movements to create a novel solidarity-based autonomous state in Rojava. The Rojavan Kurds reject the nation-state model, which, since its foundation, has been based on the 'othering' of non-native ethnic minorities. As Evangelos Aretaios (2015) describes:

> In Rojava, many different religious and ethnic groups – Christians, Yezidis, Arabs, Turkmens, Chechens, Armenians – live together with the large Kurdish majority. By officially and insistently denying the nation state and by trying to create administrative structures that incorporate these different elements, the Rojava model gives to minorities a participatory role unprecedented in the Middle East – a role as equals in the management of the *polis*.[9]

The Rojova autonomous region has established gender equality as an organising principle. Every institution and organisation has a 40 per cent quota of representation for women, 40 per cent for men and the remaining 20 per cent for whichever sex receives the higher number of votes. 'From the smallest local organization to the parliament and government, this 40% quota is imposed and in many cases there is an obligation to have women as co-presidents or vice-presidents.'

10 *Culture as development*

Cultural production and participation under capitalism is based upon a dual process of degradation (of indigenous and working-class cultures) and then its repackaging and commodification for sale for profit. Under capitalism, culture is established as a separate sphere (of leisure activity) divorced from social reproductive activities. Through commodification, culture becomes a mark of distinction and class differentiation (Bourdieu 1984), whereas before degradation/ commodification it represented a form of, and forum for, (community) participation. Cultural development will fortify the social ownership and control of the means of production and the democratic identification of needs.

Cultural development will be facilitated, in part, through advanced education for all, based upon a radical pedagogy of the oppressed and conscientisation. Conscientisation is 'the process in which men [and women], not as recipients, but as knowing subjects, achieve a deepening awareness both of the socio-cultural reality that shapes their lives and [of] their capacity to transform that reality' (Freire 1972: 51). This pedagogy will facilitate the transformation of developmental objects into developmental subjects.

State and local investments will support the integration of conscientisation-based education into the functioning of community-level participatory planning. Banking systems of education will be replaced by participatory forms. Indigenous, local, historical and cultural traditions will be used to construct new educational traditions. These traditions will contribute to cultural renewal through the de-alienation, de-fragmentation, and reintegration of social life. New television, radio, print and digital media will be established to create fora and means for the dissemination of indigenous and emergent labouring-class cultures.

These are our proposals for a new practice of socialised, participatory, democratic development. We expect fully that other proposals will be advanced and debated in the same democratic spirit.

Conclusions

Capitalism is an immensely dynamic wealth-generating system. It has established, on a global scale, the basis for a world free from poverty. This potential is the dream upon which the Millennium and Sustainable Development Goals trade. But capitalism can never realise this potential. It is a system of endless competitive capital accumulation, exploitation, oppression and environmental destruction. These social relations will more certainly wreck the planet, create new forms of mass poverty, and reproduce mega-inequalities than deliver the dream of well-being for all. The anti-poverty consensus advocates the continued expansion and deepening of capitalist social relations, which they frame, in Orwellian terms, as emancipatory.

The other side of the coin of the APC's development agenda is to eliminate, ideologically and materially, alternative conceptions and strategies of pursuing human development. The formation of an impoverished and super-exploited global labouring class is the logical outcome of the APC's world view and its institutional realisation. For these reasons, an alternative conception of human development and a means of achieving it are imperative. This book's concept of labour-led development, its argument for a radical democratisation of resource generation and political structures through the reabsorption of the state by society, and the ten-point plan outlined in this chapter aim to contribute to that alternative.

We began this book by arguing that George Orwell's concept of doublethink, from his novel *1984*, describes contemporary development discourse. *1984* represented Orwell's post-war despair at the collapse of the potential for socialist development and the emergence of rival superpowers seeking to carve up and dominate the globe. A decade or so earlier, when that potential still existed, Orwell had participated in the Spanish Civil War. He observed first-hand the atmosphere of Barcelona, which was for a brief moment a worker-controlled city:

> It was the first time that I had ever been in a town where the working class was in the saddle. . . . Waiters and shop-walkers looked you in the face and treated you as an equal. Servile and even ceremonial forms of speech had temporarily disappeared. Nobody said 'Señor' or 'Don' or even 'Usted'; everyone called everyone else 'Comrade' and 'Thou', and said 'Salud!' instead of 'Buenos dias'. . . . In outward appearance it was a town in which the wealthy classes had practically ceased to exist. All this was queer and moving. There was much in it that I did not understand, in some ways I did not even like it, but I recognized it immediately as a state of affairs worth fighting for. (Orwell [1938] 2011: ch. 1)

The power of labouring classes to forge their own forms of human development represents the only effective alternative to the double-think that plagues our deliberations about development. All forms of top-down development require that a small minority exert control over the majority of a society. In order to secure the ideological hegemony of such forms of development, these social relations of domination and exploitation need to be cloaked by mystifying ideologies supported by pseudo-scientific methods.

Democratic, collective, labour-led forms of human development are potentially able to present the social reality of the world in a clear light. Because they represent the interests of the majority, they do not need cloaking ideologies to mask the social relations that underpin their world view. Rather they depend upon highlighting capitalism's exploitative dynamics and the democratic potential of a future, non-exploitative society.

Labour-led development is a real process rather than a distant utopia. It is occurring at this moment across the world. The tasks for progressive social scientists, activists, development theorists and practitioners are to identify examples and attempts to engender LLD, and to support them, practically and theoretically. The potential for genuine transformation is captured by an organiser at one of the occupied factories discussed in chapter 5: 'This [process of factory occupation and recovery] is big, because . . . what one has regarded as a utopia, has become now necessary and possible . . . If we could take this . . . to a regional, country, world level . . . we would be talking of another world' (quoted in Aiziczon 2009: 12).

Notes

Chapter 1 The Big Lie

1 The newly established Sustainable Development Goals (SDGs) represent the latest form taken by the APC, which aims, primarily, to 'end poverty by 2030 in all its forms everywhere'. Other SDGs include ending hunger (goal 2), achieving gender equality and empowerment of all women and girls (goal 5), reducing inequality within and between countries (goal 10), combating climate change and its impacts (goal 13), and promoting peaceful and inclusive societies for sustainable development and to provide access to justice for all (goal 16). See www.un.org/sustainabledevelopment/sustainable-development-goals/.

2 Credit Suisse, *Global Wealth Report 2013*, https://publications.credit-suisse.com/tasks/render/file/?fileID=BCDB1364-A105-0560-1332EC9100FF5C83, and *Global Wealth Report 2015*, https://publications.credit-suisse.com/tasks/render/file/?fileID=F2425415-DCA7-80B8-EAD989AF9341D47E.

3 Greg Sargent, 'There's been class warfare for the last 20 years, and my class has won', 30 September 2011, www.washingtonpost.com/blogs/plum-line/post/theres-been-class-warfare-for-the-last-20-years-and-my-class-has-won/2011/03/03/gIQApaFbAL_blog.html?utm_term=.9aec1c5c08f8.

4 'World Bank forecasts global poverty to fall below 10% for first time', 4 October 2015, www.worldbank.org/en/news/press-release/2015/10/04/world-bank-forecasts-global-poverty-to-fall-below-10-for-first-time-major-hurdles-remain-in-goal-to-end-poverty-by-2030.

5 'Towards the end of poverty', *The Economist*, 1 June 2013, www.eco nomist.com/news/leaders/21578665-nearly-1-billion-people-have -been-taken-out-extreme-poverty-20-years-world-should-aim.

6 'Unbridled capitalism is the "dung of the devil", says Pope Francis', *The Guardian*, 10 July 2015, www.theguardian.com/world/2015/jul/10/poor-must-change-new-colonialism-of-economic-order-sa ys-pope-francis.

7 The term pro-labour development is borrowed from Pattenden (2016).

8 For more on the definition and meaning of class relations, how to conduct class analysis, and implications for development studies, see Campling et al. (2016).

9 See Smith (2016) for a useful account.

10 Maria Gallotti, 'Migrant domestic workers across the world: global and regional estimates', www.ilo.org/wcmsp5/groups/public/---ed_protect/---protrav/---migrant/documents/briefingnote/wc ms_490162.pdf.

11 Khadija Patel, 'Anti-immigrant violence spreads in South Africa', *Al Jazeera*, 18 April 2015, www.aljazeera.com/news/2015/04/fear-grips-foreigners-johannesburg-150417081633360.html.

12 'Chinese wages higher than Brazil, Mexico', 27 February 2017, www. chinaeconomicreview.com/chinese-wages-higher-brazil-mexico.

Chapter 2 Capitalism and Poverty

1 'Absolute low income measures the proportion of individuals who have household incomes below 60 per cent of the average in 2010/11 (chosen as a benchmark) and is adjusted for inflation.' See Joseph Rowntree Foundation, 'Relative and absolute poverty over time, 28 June 2016, www.jrf.org.uk/data/relative-and-absolute-poverty-over-time, and Department for Work & Pensions, 'Households below average income: an analysis of the UK income distribu-tion, 1994/95–2014/15', 28 June 2016, www.gov.uk/government/uploads/system/uploads/attachment_data/file/532416/househol ds-below-average-income-1994-1995-2014-2015.pdf#page=6.

2 Since the Bank has not yet provided poverty data for 2012–15, this figure is an estimate, and a weak one at that, based upon unrealistic assumptions about the relationship between growth and poverty reduction. See Sumner (2016) for an explanation of why economic growth over the last twenty-five years has yielded limited poverty reduction.

3 'World Bank forecasts global poverty to fall below 10% for first time', 4 October 2015, www.worldbank.org/en/news/press-release/2015/10/04/world-bank-forecasts-global-poverty-to-fall-below-10-for-first-time-major-hurdles-remain-in-goal-to-end-poverty-by-2030.

4 One of the biggest problems with the Bank's updates to its PPP methodology is that they are not comparable, which means that, even on its own terms, the Bank's data and pronouncements are unreliable (cf. Reddy and Pogge 2010).

5 This is important because Ravallion argues that those living at above $2 a day (2005 PPP) are now part of the emerging developing world middle class. Had the $2-a-day rate been increased in line with the lower poverty line, the growth of the middle class would be smaller than he claims (see section 2.3).

6 Mukul Devichand, 'When a dollar a day means 25 cents', 2 December 2007, http://news.bbc.co.uk/2/hi/business/7122356.stm.

7 The concept of a living wage used here derives, initially, from the United Nations' Declaration of Human Rights (1948), updated by the Clean Clothes Campaign. The Declaration's article 23 on the right to work states, among other things, that a worker is entitled to the right to 'just and favourable remuneration ensuring for himself and his family an existence worthy of human dignity'. The Clean Clothes Campaign avers that 'A living wage should be earned in a standard working week (no more than 48 hours) and allow a garment worker to be able to buy food for herself and her family, pay the rent, pay for healthcare, clothing, transportation and education and have a small amount of savings for when something unexpected happens.' It is a mark of the degradation of the developmental imagination at the hands of the APC that the measurement of global poverty cannot even be conceived in terms formulated by the United Nations over seven decades ago (see www.un.org/en/

universal-declaration-human-rights/ and 'A living wage = a human right', https://cleanclothes.org/livingwage).

8 The Asian Floor Wage Alliance, a global coalition of trade unions and workers' rights and human rights organisations, has conducted impressive research and advocacy in this direction. See Bhattacharjee and Roy (2015).

9 'Living wage versus minimum wage', 1 May 2014, https://clean clothes.org/livingwage/living-wage-versus-minimum-wage.

10 Paul Mason, 'Who are the new middle classes around the world?', *The Guardian*, 20 January 2014, www.theguardian.com/comment isfree/2014/jan/20/new-middle-classes-world-poor.

11 As Steans and Tepe (2010, 808–9) note, 'The separation of re-production and production . . . renders invisible a key dimension of power relations . . . the [de]naturalization of gender relations, attendant on such demarcations, has consequently been a key site of feminist political struggles.'

12 'Women today – the facts', *New Internationalist*, January 1992, https://newint.org/features/1992/01/05/facts/.

13 As the World Food Programme notes, 'Food has never before existed in such abundance . . . In purely quantitative terms, there is enough food available to feed the entire global population of 7 billion people' (www.wfp.org/hunger/causes).

Chapter 3 Poverty Chains and the World Economy

1 This chapter builds on previous work of the author, for example Selwyn (2007, 2008, 2012, 2013, 2015a, 2016).

2 The main thrust of this chapter concurs with the core arguments made in Smith's *Imperialism in the Twenty-First Century* (2016). I differ from Smith over his claim that Northern workers benefit from Southern workers' super-exploitation, and that super-exploitation is limited to the global South. As noted later in this chapter, the expansion of super-exploitative accumulation strategies across the global South is facilitating heightened rates of 'normal' exploitation *and* super-exploitation across the global North.

3 I thank Tony Norfield for a helpful discussion about wages and productivity.

4 It is instructive here to quote Adam Smith's observation about British manufacturers' self-portrayal: 'Our merchants frequently complain of the high wages of British labour as the cause of their manufactures being undersold in foreign markets, but they are silent about the high profits of stock. They complain of the extravagant gain of other people, but they say nothing of their own' (Smith 1976: book iv, chapter 7, part 3).

5 This section is based upon a report by Christa Luginbühl and Bettina Musiolek of the Clean Clothes Campaign. In the post-socialist countries, around 700,000 workers were formally employed and 350,000 were informally employed in 2013. In Turkey the figures were 508,000 (formally employed) and 1.5 million (informally employed) in the garment and leather industry (Luginbühl and Musiolek 2014: 14).

6 Marianela Jarroud, 'Seasonal agricultural workers left out of Chilean boom', 23 May 2014, www.ipsnews.net/2014/05/seasonal-agricultural-workers-left-chilean-boom/.

7 Jo Tuckman, 'Baja California farm workers demand better pay and working conditions', *The Guardian*, 25 March 2015, www.theguardian.com/world/2015/mar/25/mexico-baja-california-farm-workers-strike, and Josh Rushing, 'Strawberry pickers strain to see fruits of their labor, even after strike', *Al Jazeera*, 21 June 2015, http://america.aljazeera.com/articles/2015/6/21/strawberry-pickers-strain-to-see-fruits-of-their-labor.html.

8 Hours of Work (Commerce and Offices) Convention, 1930, www.ilo.org/dyn/normlex/en/f?p=NORMLEXPUB:12100:0::NO:1210 0:P12100_INSTRUMENT_ID:312175:NO.

9 Drew Desilver, 'For most workers, real wages have barely budged for decades', 9 October 2014, www.pewresearch.org/fact-tank/2014/10/09/for-most-workers-real-wages-have-barely-budged-for-decades/.

10 Leslie Kwoh, '"Rank and yank" retains vocal fans', *Wall Street Journal*, 31 January 2012, www.wsj.com/news/articles/SB1000142 405297020336350457718 6970064375222.

Chapter 4 Deepening Exploitation

1 The concepts of primary and secondary agency are derived from Hobson (2012).
2 Friedrich Hayek, letter to *The Times* of London, 3 August 1978. See Selwyn (2015b) for a discussion of Hayek's logically connected promotion of free-market capitalism and opposition to any form of meaningful popular democracy.
3 Since the advent of the global economic crisis, it seems that there is a shift back towards a harder Washington Consensus-style approach to labour. In the global North this is taking the form of austerity economics, and in the global South (in particular in Latin America), following the collapse of the commodity super-cycle, earlier attempts to 'include' labour in development are being sidelined.
4 Joseph E. Stiglitz, 'China's roadmap', 6 April, 2006, www.project-syndicate.org/commentary/china-s-roadmap?barrier=true.
5 See 'Decent work', www.ilo.org/global/topics/decent-work/lang--en/index.htm.
6 For a detailed discussion of the evolution and different strands of statist political economy, see Selwyn (2014: chs 2 and 4).
7 For example, Hagen Koo writes that, in 2014, 'approximately one third of South Korean workers suffer from insecure job conditions, receiving only around 60 per cent of regular workers' wages with no medical insurance, severance pay or company welfare subsidies.' See Hagen Koo, 'Inequality in South Korea', 1 July 2014, www.eastasiaforum.org/2014/07/01/inequality-in-south-korea/.

Chapter 5 Resisting Exploitation

1 This section draws on Michael Lebowitz (2003).
2 Expanded leisure time should be a core goal of advocates of alternative/progressive development. The Oxford English Dictionary includes the following definition of leisure: 'Opportunity afforded by free time to do something' (www.oxforddictionaries.com/defi

nition/english/leisure). The etymological roots of the word 'leisure', extending back to Latin and Old French, emphasise how the concept refers to opportunities to do things, freedom, ease and peace.

3 'The rising power of the Chinese worker', *The Economist*, 29 July 2010, www.economist.com/node/16693333. 'Chinese wages higher than Brazil, Mexico', 27 February 2017, www.chinaeconomicreview. com/chinese-wages-higher-brazil-mexico.

4 This section draws on Hauf (2016).

Chapter 6 Beyond Exploitation

1 The following builds upon Lebowitz (2015: 183–4).

2 James S. Henry, *The Price of Offshore Revisited: New Estimates for 'Missing' Global Private Wealth, Income, Inequality, and Lost Taxes*, July 2012, www.taxjustice.net/cms/upload/pdf/Price_of_ Offshore_Revisited_26072012.pdf. See also Nicholas Shaxson, John Christensen and Nick Mathiason, *Inequality: You Don't Know the Half of It (or Why Inequality is Worse than We Thought)*, July 2012, www.taxjustice.net/cms/upload/pdf/Inequality_120722_ You_dont_know_the_half_of_it.pdf, and James K. Boyce and Léonce Ndikumana, 'African debt: funny money and stolen lives', 28 September 2011, http://africanarguments.org/2011/09/28/ african-debt-funny-money-and-stolen-lives-by-james-k-boyce- and-leonce-ndikumana/.

3 Pranab Bardhan, 'Could a basic income help poor countries?', 22 June 2016, www.project-syndicate.org/commentary/developing- country-basic-income-by-pranab-bardhan-2016-06.

4 The Freedom Charter, 26 June 1955, www.sahistory.org.za/article/ freedom-charter.

5 People's Agreement of Cochabamba, 22 April 2010, https://pwccc. wordpress.com/2010/04/24/peoples-agreement/.

6 Climate Justice Now! statement, 3 November 2008, www.carbon tradewatch.org/index.php?option=com_content&task=view&id=2 27&Itemid=95.

7 For example, we will seek to work with movements such as Divest

London to reorientate divested finances into new, progressive activities; http://divestlondon.org/.

8 These principles are adapted from those established by the Bolivarian Alliance for the Peoples of Our America; see http://alba-tcp.org/en/contenido/principles-alba.

9 Evangelos Aretaios, 'The Rojava revolution', 15 March 2015, www.opendemocracy.net/arab-awakening/evangelos-aretaios/rojava-revolution.

References

Acker, J. (2004) 'Gender, capitalism and globalization', *Critical Sociology*, 30(1): 17–41.

Aiziczon, F. (2009) *Zanón: una experiencia de lucha obrera*. Buenos Aires: Herramienta.

Akram-Lodhi, H. (2015) 'Accelerating towards food sovereignty', *Third World Quarterly*, 36(3): 563–83.

Alexander, P., T. Lekgowa, B. Mmope, L. Sinwell and B. Xezwi (2013) *Marikana: Voices from South Africa's Mining Massacre*. Athens: Ohio University Press.

Ali, M. (2016) 'Dark matter, black holes and old-fashioned exploitation: transnational corporations and the US economy', *Cambridge Journal of Economics*, 40: 997–1018.

Altvater, E. (2007) 'The social and natural environment of fossil capitalism', in L. Panitch and C. Leys (eds) *Socialist Register 2007: Coming to Terms with Nature*, pp. 37–59.

Amsden, A. (1989) *Asia's Next Giant: South Korea and Late Industrialization*. Oxford: Oxford University Press.

Amsden, A. (1990) 'Third world industrialization: "global Fordism" or a new model?', *New Left Review*, 182: 5.

Apple Inc. (2014) *Supplier Responsibility: 2014 Progress Report*, www.apple.com/supplier-responsibility/pdf/Apple_SR_2014_Progress_Report.pdf.

Arnold, D. (2013) *Workers' Agency and Re-Working Power Relations in Cambodia's Garment Industry*, Capturing the Gains working paper 24. Manchester: Capturing the Gains, University of Manchester, www.capturingthegains.org/pdf/ctg-wp-2013-24.pdf.

Atzeni, M., and P. Ghigliani (2007) 'Labour process and decision-making in factories under workers' self-management: empirical evidence from Argentina', *Work, Employment and Society*, 21(4): 653–71.

Bacon, D. (2015) 'The Pacific coast farm-worker rebellion', *The Nation*, 28 August, www.thenation.com/article/the-pacific-coast-farm-worker-rebellion/.

Bair, J. (2010) 'On difference and capital: gender and the globalization of production', *Signs*, 36(1): 203–26.

Bakker, I., and S. Gill (eds) (2003) *Power, Production and Social Reproduction: Human In/security in the Global Political Economy*. Basingstoke: Palgrave Macmillan.

Banerjee, A. V., and E. Duflo (2007) *What is Middle Class about the Middle Classes around the World?*, MIT Department of Economics working paper, no. 07-29, http://economics.mit.edu/files/2081.

Bannerji, H. (1995) *Thinking Through: Essays on Feminism, Marxism and Anti-Racism*. Toronto: Women's Press.

Barker, C. (1998) 'Industrialism, capitalism, value, force and states: some theoretical remarks', Anglo-Bulgarian Comparative History Seminar, Wolverhampton University; https://sites.google.com/site/colinbarkersite/5---publications-and-papers-1996-2000.

Basu, K. (2016) 'The world economy's labor pains', Project Syndicate, 4 January, www.project-syndicate.org.

Benya, A. (2015) 'The invisible hands: women in Marikana', *Review of African Political Economy*, 42(146): 545–60.

Bernstein, H. (2010) *Class Dynamics of Agrarian Change*. Sterling, VA: Kumarian Press.

Bhattacharjee, A., and A. Roy (2015) 'Bargaining in the global commodity chain: the Asia Floor Wage Alliance', in K. van der Pijl (ed.) *Handbook of the International Political Economy of Production*. Cheltenham: Edward Elgar, pp. 334–51.

Binns, P., and M. Gonzalez (1980) 'Cuba, Castro and socialism', *International Socialism Journal*, 2(8): 1–36.

Birkinshaw, M. (2008) 'A big devil in the shacks: the politics of fire', *Pambazuka News*, 17 September, www.pambazuka.org/governance/big-devil-shacks.

Boggs, C. (1977) 'Marxism, prefigurative communism, and the problem of workers' control', *Radical America*, 11(6): 99–122.

Boltvinik, J., and A. Damián (2016) 'Irrelevance of the MDGs and a real solution to poverty: Universal Citizen's Income', in D. Cimadamore, G. Koehler and T. Pogge (eds) *Poverty and the Millennium Development Goals: A Critical Look Forward*. London: Zed Books, pp. 173–202.

Bond, P. (2012) 'How the Marikana movement stunned neoliberal South Africa', *Counterpunch*, 19 October, www.counterpunch.org/2012/10/19/how-the-marikana-movement-stunned-neoliberal-south-africa/.

Bourdieu, P. (1984) *Distinction*. Abingdon: Routledge.

Branford, S., and J. Rocha (2002) *Cutting the Wire: The Story of the Landless Movement in Brazil*. London: Latin American Bureau.

Brenner, R. (1986) 'The social basis of economic development', in J. Roemer (ed.) *Analytical Marxism*. Cambridge: Cambridge University Press, pp. 23–53.

Breslin, S. (2011) 'The "China model" and the global crisis: from Friedrich List to a Chinese mode of governance?', *International Affairs*, 87(6): 1323–43.

Brown, J. (2014) 'Abahlali's choice', *Daily Maverick*, 4 May, www.dailymaverick.co.za/article/2014-05-04-5365753498943/#.Vo5NflKfYXI.

Brzezinski, Z. (2007) *Second Chance: Three Presidents and the Crisis of the American Superpower*. New York: Basic Books.

Buccus, I. (2009) 'Durban breaks new ground in participatory democracy', *Mail and Guardian*, 12 March, http://thoughtleader.co.za/imraanbuccus/2009/03/12/durban-breaks-new-ground-in-participatory-democracy/.

CAFOD (2004) *Clean up your Computer: Working Conditions in the Electronics Sector*. London: CAFOD; http://goodelectronics.org/publications-en/Publication_854.

Camfield, D. (2016) 'Elements of a historical-materialist theory of racism', *Historical Materialism*, 24(1): 31–70.

Cammack, P. (2002) 'Attacking the global poor', *New Left Review*, 13: 125.

Cammack, P. (2013) *Socio-Economic Rights in the World Market: China, India, and the Gang of Four*, Multilateral Development Banks and the Global Financial Crisis working paper series. Hong Kong: City University.

Campling, L., S. Miyamura, J. Pattenden and B. Selwyn (2016) 'Class dynamics of development: a methodological note', *Third World Quarterly*, 37(10): 1745-67.

Capps, G. (2015) 'Labour in the time of platinum', *Review of African Political Economy*, 42(146): 497-507.

Carballo, A. (2016) Empowering development: capabilities and Latin American critical traditions, PhD thesis, University of Westminster.

Carswell, G., and G. De Neve (2014) 'MGNREGA in Tamil Nadu: a story of success and transformation?', *Journal of Agrarian Change*, 14(4): 564-85.

Chan, S., and D. Kwan (2003) 'Union's new approach puts workers' rights first', *South China Morning Post*, 12 September.

Chang, D.-O. (2002) 'Korean labour relations in transition: authoritarian flexibility?', *Labour, Capital and Society/Travail, capital et société*, 35(1): 10-40.

Chang, H.-J. (2002) *Kicking Away the Ladder: Development Strategy in Historical Perspective*. London: Anthem Press.

Chang, H.-J., and I. Grabel (2004) *Reclaiming Development: An Alternative Economic Policy Manual*. London: Zed Books.

China Labor Watch (2015) *Analyzing Labor Conditions of Pegatron and Foxconn: Apple's Low-Cost Reality*, CLW Report 107, www.chinal aborwatch.org/report/107.

China Labour Bulletin (2012) *A Decade of Change: The Workers' Movement in China 2000-2010*. Hong Kong: China Labour Bulletin; www.clb.org.hk/sites/default/files/archive/en/File/research_rep orts/Decade%20of%20the%20Workers%20Movement%20final.pdf.

China Labour Bulletin (2014) *Searching for the Union: The Workers' Movement in China 2011-13*. Hong Kong: China Labour Bulletin; www.clb.org.hk/sites/default/files/archive/en/File/research_repor ts/searching%20for%20the%20union%201.pdf.

Chomsky, N. (1991) *Deterring Democracy*. London: Verso.

Cimadamore, D., G. Koehler and T. Pogge (2016) 'Poverty and the Millennium Development Goals: a critical look forward', in D. Cimadamore, G. Koehler and T. Pogge (eds) *Poverty and the*

Millennium Development Goals: A Critical Look Forward. London: Zed Books, pp. 3–25.

Clark, B., and J. B. Foster (2009) 'Ecological imperialism and the global metabolic rift: unequal exchange and the guano/nitrates trade', *International Journal of Comparative Sociology*, 50(3–4): 311–34.

Clark, T. D. (2015) 'Class transformations in Chile's capitalist revolution', *Socialist Register*, 51: 199–215.

Cleaver, H. (2000) *Reading Capital Politically*. Leeds: Antithesis Press.

Clelland, D. (2014) 'The core of the apple: degrees of monopoly and dark value in global commodity chains', *Journal of World-Systems Research*, 20(1): 82–111.

Cliff, T. (1987) 'Workers' revolution and beyond', in P. Binns, T. Cliff and C. Harman, *Russia: From Workers' State to State Capitalism*. London: Bookmarks, pp. 7–12.

Cliff, T. (1974) *State Capitalism in Russia*. London: Pluto Press.

Cliff, T., and D. Gluckstein (1996) *The Labour Party: A Marxist History*. London: Bookmarks.

Cohen, G. A. (1978) *Karl Marx's Theory of History*. Oxford: Oxford University Press.

Conroy, M., D. Murray and P. Rosset (1996) *A Cautionary Tale: Failed US Development Policy in Central America*. Boulder, CO: Lynne Rienner.

Cowen, M., and R. Shenton (1996) *Doctrines of Development*. London: Routledge.

Crotty, J., and G. Epstein (1996) 'In defence of capital controls', *Socialist Register*, 32: 118–49.

Davidson, N. (2013) 'The neoliberal era in Britain: historical developments and current perspectives', *International Socialism*, no. 139: 171–223.

Daviron, B., and S. Ponte (2005) *The Coffee Paradox: Global Markets, Commodity Trade and the Elusive Promise of Development*. London: Zed Books.

Davis, M. (2006) *Planet of Slums*. London: Verso.

Desai, M. (2002) *Marx's Revenge: The Resurgence of Capitalism and the Death of Statist Socialism*. London: Verso.

Deutscher, I. (1967) *Stalin: A Political Biography*. Rev edn, Harmondsworth: Penguin.

Dicken, P. (2011) *Global Shift: Mapping the Changing Contours of the World Economy*. 6th edn, London: Sage.

Dinerstein, A. C. (2010) 'Autonomy in Latin America: between resistance and integration: echoes from the *Piqueteros* experience', *Community Development Journal*, 45(3): 356–66.

Dinerstein, A. C. (2015) *The Politics of Autonomy in Latin America: The Art of Organising Hope*. Basingstoke: Palgrave Macmillan.

Draper, H. (1966) *The Two Souls of Socialism*. Highland Park, MI: International Socialists.

Du Bois, W. E. B. ([1935] 2013) *Black Reconstruction in America: Toward a History of the Part which Black Folk Played in the Attempt to Reconstruct Democracy in America, 1860–1880*. New Brunswick, NJ: Transaction.

Dunaway, W. A. (2014) 'Bringing commodity chain analysis back to its world-systems roots: rediscovering women's work and households', *Journal of World-Systems Research*, 20(1): 64–81.

Eagleton, T. (2011) *Why Marx was Right*. New Haven, CT: Yale University Press.

Edward, P. (2006) 'The ethical poverty line: a moral quantification of absolute poverty', *Third World Quarterly*, 27(2): 377–93.

Elias, J., and S. Gunawardana (eds) (2013) *The Global Political Economy of the Household in Asia*. Basingstoke: Palgrave Macmillan.

Elliot, P. (2006) 'Zanon Workers in Argentina Still Waiting for Security', *Upside Down World*, 27 June, http://upsidedownworld.org/main/argentina-archives-32/336-zanon-workers-in-argentina-still-waiting-for-security.

Elson, D. (1988) 'Market socialism or socialization of the market?', *New Left Review*, 172: 3.

Elson, D. (1994) 'Micro, meso, macro: gender and economic analysis in the context of policy reform', in Isabella Bakker (ed.) *The Strategic Silence: Gender and Economic Policy*. London: Zed Books.

Elson, D., and R. Pearson (1981) 'Nimble fingers make cheap workers: an analysis of women's employment in third world export manufacturing', *Quarterly Feminist Review*, 7: 87–101.

Epsom, M. (2016) 'Food, agriculture and climate change', *International Socialism*, no. 152; http://isj.org.uk/food-agriculture-and-climate-change/#footnote-10080-15-backlink.

Esteva, G. (1992) 'Development', in W. Sachs (ed.) *The Development Dictionary*. London: Zed Books, pp. 6–25.

Evans, P. (1995) *Embedded Autonomy: States and Industrial Transformation*. Princeton, NJ: Princeton University Press.

FAO [Food and Agricultural Organization] (2012) *The State of Food Insecurity in the World*. Rome: FAO.

Federici, S. (2004) *Caliban and the Witch*. New York: Autonomedia.

Ferguson, S. (2008) 'Canadian contributions to social reproduction feminism, race and embodied labor', *Race, Gender & Class*, 15(1–2): 42–57.

Ferguson, S., and D. McNally (2015) 'Precarious migrants: gender, race and the social reproduction of a global working class', *Socialist Register*, 51: 1–23.

Fishwick, A., and B. Selwyn (2016) 'Labour-centred development in Latin America: two cases of alternative development', *Geoforum*, 74: 233–43.

Flassbeck, H., and C. Lapavitsas (2015) *Against the Troika: Crisis and Austerity in the Eurozone*. London: Verso.

Foster, J. B., and R. W. McChesney (2012) 'The global stagnation and China', *Monthly Review*, 63(9): 3–21.

Freire, P. (1972) *Pedagogy of the Oppressed*. New York: Penguin.

Friedman, E. (2014) 'Alienated politics: labour insurgency and the paternalistic state in China', *Development and Change*, 45(5): 1001–18.

Fuchs, C. (2016) 'Digital labour and imperialism', *Monthly Review*, 67(8): 1–9; http://monthlyreview.org/2016/01/01/digital-labor-and-imperialism/.

Garvey, B., D. Tyfield and L. Freire de Mello (2015) '"Meet the new boss . . . same as the old boss?" Technology, toil and tension in the agro-fuel frontier', *New Technology, Work and Employment*, 30(2): 79–94.

Geras, N. (2000) 'Minimum utopia: ten theses', *Socialist Register*, 36: 41–52.

Gibson, N. (2011) *Fanonian Practices in South Africa: From Steve Biko to Abahlali baseMjondolo*. New York: Palgrave Macmillan.

Giddens, A. (2009) *Sociology*. 6th edn, Cambridge: Polity.

Gills, B., and J. Rocamora (1992) 'Low intensity democracy', *Third World Quarterly*, 13(3): 501–23.

Gowan, P. (1999) *The Global Gamble: Washington's Faustian Bid for World Dominance*. London: Verso.

Gray, K. (2014) *Labour and Development in East Asia: Social Forces and Passive Revolution*. Abingdon: Routledge.

Gwynne R. N. (1999) 'Globalisation, commodity chains and fruit exporting regions in Chile', *Tijdschrift voor economische en sociale geografie*, 90(2): 211–25.

Hammer, N., R. Plugor, P. Nolan and I. Clark (2015) *New Industry on a Skewed Playing Field: Supply Chain Relations and Working Conditions in UK Garment Manufacturing*. Leicester: University of Leicester, Centre for Sustainable Work and Employment Futures.

Hanlon, J., A. Barrientos and D. Hulme (2012) *Just Give Money to the Poor: The Development Revolution from the Global South*. Sterling, VA: Kumarian Press.

Hardoon, D., R. Fuentes-Nieva and S. Ayele (2016) *An Economy for the 1%: How Privilege and Power in the Economy Drive Extreme Inequality and How This Can Be Stopped*. Oxford: Oxfam.

Hardt, M., and A. Negri (2000) *Empire*. Cambridge, MA: Harvard University Press.

Harman, C. (1974) *Bureaucracy and Revolution in Eastern Europe*. London: Bookmarks.

Harman, C. (1999) *A People's History of the World*. London: Bookmarks.

Harman, C. (2002a) 'Argentina: rebellion at the sharp end of the world crisis', *International Socialism*, no. 94: 1–35.

Harman, C. (2002b) 'The workers of the world', *International Socialism*, no. 96: 3–46.

Harnecker, M. (2014) 'Decentralised participatory planning based on experiences of Brazil, Venezuela and the state of Kerala, India', *Links: International Journal of Socialist Renewal*, http://links.org.au/node/4208.

Harris, N. (1978) *The Mandate of Heaven: Marx and Mao in Modern China*. London: Quartet.

Harris, N. (1987) *The End of the Third World: Newly Industrialising Countries and the Decline of an Ideology*. Harmondsworth: Penguin.

Harriss-White, B. (2006) 'Poverty and capitalism', *Economic & Political Weekly*, 41(13): 1241–6.

Harvey, D. (1996) *Justice, Nature and the Geography of Difference*. Oxford: Blackwell.

Hauf, F. (2016) *Beyond Decent Work: The Cultural Political Economy of Labour Struggles in Indonesia*. Frankfurt am Main: Campus.

Henwood, D. (1995). 'Clinton's trade policy', in F. Rosen and D. McFadyen (eds) *Free Trade and Economic Restructuring in Latin America*. New York: Monthly Review Press.

Hickel, J. (2016) 'The true extent of global poverty and hunger: questioning the good news narrative of the Millennium Development Goals', *Third World Quarterly*, 37(5): 749–67.

Hickey, S., and G. Mohan (2004) *Participation – from Tyranny to Transformation? Exploring New Approaches to Participation in Development*. London: Zed Books.

Hite, A., and J. S. Viterna (2005) 'Gendering class in Latin America: how women effect and experience change in the class structure', *Latin American Research Review*, 40(2): 50–82.

Hobson, J. M. (2012) *The Eurocentric Conception of World Politics: Western International Theory, 1760–2010*. Cambridge: Cambridge University Press.

Hoff, K., and J. Stiglitz (2001) 'Modern economic theory and development', in *Frontiers of Development Economics*. Washington, DC: World Bank, pp. 389–459.

Holloway, J. (2002) *Change the World without Taking Power*. London: Pluto Press.

Holt-Giménez, E. (2002) 'Measuring farmers' agroecological resistance after Hurricane Mitch in Nicaragua: a case study in participatory, sustainable land management impact monitoring', *Agriculture, Ecosystems & Environment*, 93(1): 87–105.

Hoskyns, C., and Rai, S. (2007) 'Recasting the global political economy: counting women's unpaid work', *New Political Economy*, 12(3): 297–317.

Hoy, C., and A. Sumner (2016) 'Global poverty and inequality: is there new capacity for redistribution in developing countries?', *Journal of Globalization and Development*, 7(1): 117–57.

Huanacuni, M. (2010) *Vivir bien/buen vivir*. La Paz: Instituto Internacional de Integración.

Human Rights Watch (2015) *'Work Faster or Get Out': Labor Rights Abuses in Cambodia's Garment Industry*, www.hrw.org/report/2015/03/11/work-faster-or-get-out/labor-rights-abuses-cambodias-garment-industry.

Huntington, S. (2006) *Political Order in Changing Societies*. New Haven, CT: Yale University Press.

ILO [International Labour Organization] (2008) 'Population and Economically Active Population, 1995–2005', *Key Indicators of the Labour Market* (5th edn, Geneva: ILO).

ILO [International Labour Organization] (2014) *Developing with Jobs*, World of Work Report. Geneva: International Labour Organization.

IMF [International Monetary Fund] (2007) *World Economic Outlook, April 2007: Spillovers and Cycles in the Global Economy*. Washington, DC: IMF; www.imf.org/external/pubs/ft/weo/2007/01/pdf/text.pdf.

Jessop, B. (2008) *State Power: A Strategic-Relational Approach*. Cambridge: Polity.

Joekes, S. P. (1987) *Women in the World Economy*. Oxford: Oxford University Press.

Johnson, C. (1982) *MITI and the Japanese Miracle*. Stanford, CA: Stanford University Press.

Jomo, K. S. (2001) 'Rethinking the role of government policy in Southeast Asia', in J. E. Stiglitz and S. Yusuf (eds) *Rethinking the East Asian Miracle*. Washington, DC: World Bank, pp. 461–508.

Jones, S. (2014) 'Tropical forests illegally destroyed for commercial agriculture', *The Guardian*, 11 September, www.theguardian.com/global-development/2014/sep/11/tropical-forests-illegally-destroyed-commercial-agriculture.

Kabeer, N. (2003) *Gender Mainstreaming in Poverty Eradication and the Millennium Development Goals: A Handbook for Policy-Makers and other Stakeholders*. Ottawa: International Development Research Centre.

Kabeer, N., and S. Mahmud (2004) 'Globalization, gender and poverty:

Bangladeshi women workers in export and local markets', *Journal of International Development*, 16(1): 93–109.

Kapsos, S. (2007) *World and Regional Trends in Labour Force Participation: Methodologies and Key Results*. Geneva: International Labour Organization.

Kapsos, S., and E. Bourmpoula (2013) *Employment and Economic Class in the Developing World*, ILO Research Paper no. 6. Geneva: International Labour Office.

Katz, L. F., and A. B. Krueger (2016) *The Rise and Nature of Alternative Work Arrangements in the United States, 1995–2015*, https://krueger.princeton.edu/sites/default/files/akrueger/files/katz_krueger_cws_-_march_29_20165.pdf.

Kerswell, T. (2013) 'Productivity and wages: what grows for workers without power and institutions', *Social Change*, 43(4): 507–31.

Keucheyan, R. (2016) *Nature is a Battlefield: Towards a Political Ecology*. Cambridge: Polity.

Kitching, G. (2001) *Seeking Social Justice through Globalization: Escaping a Nationalist Perspective*. University Park: Penn State University Press.

Klein, N. (2008) *The Shock Doctrine: The Rise of Disaster Capitalism*. New York: Picador.

Kloppenburg, J. (2010) 'Impeding dispossession, enabling repossession: biological open source and the recovery of seed sovereignty', *Journal of Agrarian Change*, 10(3): 367–88.

Kohli, A. (2004) *State-Directed Development: Political Power and Industrialization in the Global Periphery*. Cambridge: Cambridge University Press.

Kraemer, K. L., G. Linden and J. Dedrick (2011) 'Capturing value in global networks: Apple's iPad and iPhone', http://pcic.merage. uci. edu/papers/2011/value_iPad_iPhone.pdf.

Kreuger, A. O. (2007) *Trade and Employment in Developing Countries*, Vol. 3: *Synthesis and Conclusions*. Chicago: University of Chicago Press.

Lanz, R., and S. Miroudot (2011) *Intra-Firm Trade: Patterns, Determinants and Policy Implications*, OECD Trade Policy Papers no. 114, www.oecd-ilibrary.org/trade/intra-firm-trade_5kg9p39lrwnn-en.

Laslett, B., and J. Brenner (1989) 'Gender and social reproduction: historical perspectives', *Annual Review of Sociology*, 15: 381–404.

Lavaca Collective (2004) *Sin Patrón: Stories from Argentina's Worker-Run Factories*. Chicago: Haymarket Books.

Lebowitz, M. (2003) *Beyond Capital: Marx's Political Economy of the Working Class*. 2nd edn, Basingstoke: Palgrave Macmillan.

Lebowitz, M. (2010) *The Socialist Alternative: Real Human Development*. New York: Monthly Review Press.

Lebowitz, M. (2015) *The Socialist Imperative: From Gotha to Now*. New York: New York University Press.

Levy, C. (2011) 'Ocupando o centro da cidade: movimento dos cortiços e ação coletiva', *Otra Economia*, 5(8): 73–96.

Lievens, M. (2010) 'Towards an eco-Marxism', *Radical Philosophy Review*, 13(1): 1–17.

López-Calva, L., and E. Ortiz-Juarez (2014) 'A vulnerability approach to the definition of the middle class', *Journal of Economic Inequality*, 12(1): 23–47.

Lucas, K. (2001) 'Brazil's landless workers' movement: "Here we are all leaders"', *International Viewpoint*, no. 333: 31–2.

Luginbühl, C., and B. Musiolek (2014) *Stitched Up: Poverty Wages for Garment Workers in Eastern Europe and Turkey*. Clean Clothes Campaign, www.cleanclothes.org/resources/publications/stitched-up-1.

Luxton, M., and K. Bezanson (2006) *Social Reproduction: Feminist Political Economy Challenges Neo-Liberalism*. Montreal: McGill-Queen's University Press.

McMichael, P. (ed.) (1994) *The Global Restructuring of Agro-Food Systems*. Ithaca, NY: Cornell University Press.

McMichael, P. (2000) *Development and Social Change: A Global Perspective*. 2nd edn, Thousand Oaks, CA: Pine Forge Press.

McMichael, P. (2009) 'A food regime analysis of the "world food crisis"', *Agriculture and Human Values*, 26(4): 281–95.

McMullen, A. (2013) *Shop 'til They Drop: Fainting and Malnutrition in Garment Workers in Cambodia*, Clean Clothes Campaign, www.cleanclothes.org/resources/national-cccs/shop-til-they-drop.

McNally, D. (2015) 'The dialectics of unity and difference in the constitution of wage-labour: on internal relations and working-class formation', *Capital & Class*, 39(1): 131–46.

Magdoff, F., and J. B. Foster (2010) 'What every environmentalist needs to know about capitalism', *Monthly Review*, 61(10), http:// monthlyreview.org/2010/03/01/what-every-environmentalist-need s-to-know-about-capitalism/.

Malm, A. (2016) *Fossil Capital: The Rise of Steam Power and the Roots of Global Warming*. London: Verso.

Mandel, E. (2002) *An Introduction to Marxist Economic Theory*. Chippendale, NSW: Resistance Books.

Marois, T. (2012) *States, Banks and Crisis: Emerging Finance Capitalism in Mexico and Turkey*. Cheltenham: Edward Elgar.

Martinez-Alier, J. (2003) *The Environmentalism of the Poor: A Study of Ecological Conflicts and Valuation*. Cheltenham: Edward Elgar.

Marx, K. (1864) Inaugural Address of the International Working Men's Association: 'The First International', www.marxists.org/archive/ marx/works/1864/10/27.htm.

Marx, K. ([1871] 1966) *The Civil War in France*. Peking: Foreign Languages Press; 1st draft, www.marxists.org/archive/marx/works/ 1871/civil-war-france/drafts/index.htm.

Marx, K. ([1867] 1990) *Capital: A Critique of Political Economy*, Vol. 1. London: Penguin.

Marx, K. ([1939] 1993) *Grundrisse: Foundations of the Critique of Political Economy* (rough draft). London: Penguin.

Marx, K., and F. Engels ([1932] 1970) *The German Ideology*. London: Lawrence & Wishart.

Mason, P. (2016) *Postcapitalism: A Guide to our Future*. New York: Macmillan.

Mazzucato, M. (2013) *The Entrepreneurial State: Debunking Public vs. Private Sector Myths*. London: Anthem Press.

Mellor, M. (2005) 'The politics of money and credit as a route to eco-logical sustainability and economic democracy', *Capitalism Nature Socialism*, 16(2): 45–60.

Mellor, M. (2012) 'Money as a public resource for development', *Development*, 55(1): 45–53.

Meyer, L., and M. Chaves (2009) 'Winds of freedom: an Argentine factory under workers' control', *Socialism and Democracy*, 23(3): 167–79.

Mezzadri, A. (2016) 'Class, gender and the sweatshop: on the nexus between labour commodification and exploitation', *Third World Quarterly*, 37(10): 1877–900.

Mies, M. (1998) *Patriarchy and Accumulation on a World Scale: Women in the International Division of Labour*. Basingstoke: Palgrave Macmillan.

Milanović, B. (2011) *Worlds Apart: Measuring International and Global Inequality*. Princeton, NJ: Princeton University Press.

Milberg, W. (2008) 'Shifting sources and uses of profits: sustaining US financialization with global value chains', *Economy and Society*, 37(3): 420–51.

Miraftab, F. (2006) 'Feminist praxis, citizenship and informal politics: reflections on South Africa's anti-eviction campaign', *International Feminist Journal of Politics*, 8(2): 194–218.

Mohanty, C. T. (2003) '"Under western eyes" revisited: feminist solidarity through anticapitalist struggles', *Signs*, 28(2): 499–535.

Moore, J. W. (2015) *Capitalism in the Web of Life: Ecology and the Accumulation of Capital*. London: Verso.

Moseley, L. (2008) 'Workers' rights in open economies: global production and domestic institutions in the developing world', *Comparative Political Studies*, 41(4–5): 674–714.

Ndikumana, L., and J. K. Boyce (2011) *Africa's Odious Debts: How Foreign Loans and Capital Flight Bled a Continent*. London: Zed Books.

Ness, I. (2016) *Southern Insurgency*. London: Pluto Press.

Ngai, P., and J. Chan (2012) 'Global capital, the state, and Chinese workers: the Foxconn experience', *Modern China*, 38(4): 383–410.

Nolan, P. (2003) 'Industrial policy in the early 21st century: the challenge of the global business revolution', in H.-J. Chang (ed.) *Rethinking Development Economics*. London: Anthem Press, pp. 299–322.

Nolan, P. (2014) 'Globalisation and industrial policy: the case of China', *The World Economy*, 37(6): 747–64.

Norfield, T. (2012) 'T-shirt economics: labour in the imperialist world economy', http://column.global-labour-university.org/2012/08/t-shirt-economics-labour-in-imperialist.html.

Norfield, T. (2014) 'T-shirt economics update', http://economicsofim perialism.blogspot.co.uk/2014/09/t-shirt-economics-update.html.

ODI [Overseas Development Institute] (2008) *Pro-Poor Growth and Development*, Briefing Paper. London: ODI.

Orwell, G. ([1949] 1977) *1984*. London: Penguin.

Orwell, G. ([1938] 2011) *Homage to Catalonia*. London: Penguin.

Oxfam (2002) *Mugged: Poverty in Your Coffee Cup*, www.oxfamamer ica.org/static/oa3/files/mugged-full-report.pdf.

Oxfam (2017) *An Economy for the 99%: It's Time to Build a Human Economy that Benefits Everyone, Not Just the Privileged Few*, www. oxfam.org/en/research/economy-99.

Panitch, L., C. Leys, G. Albo and D. Coates (2001) 'Preface', in L. Panich and C. Leys (eds) *The Socialist Register*, 37: vii–xi.

Pattenden, J. (2016) *Labour, State and Society in Rural India: A Class-Relational Approach*. Oxford: Oxford University Press.

Pearson, R. (2000) 'All change? Men, women and reproductive work in the global economy', *European Journal of Development Research*, 12(2): 219–37.

Peck, J., and A. Tickell (2002) 'Neoliberalizing space', *Antipode*, 34(3): 380–404.

Petras, J. (2002) 'The unemployed workers movement in Argentina', *Monthly Review*, 53(8): 1–12.

Pickles, J. (2012) *Economic and Social Upgrading in Apparel Global Value Chains: Public Governance and Trade Policy*, Capturing the Gains working paper 13, www.capturingthegains.org/pdf/ctg-wp-2012-13.pdf.

Piketty, T. (2014) *Capital in the Twenty-First Century*. Cambridge, MA: Harvard University Press.

Pithouse, R. (2006) 'Struggle is a school: the rise of a shack dwellers' movement in Durban, South Africa', *Monthly Review*, 57(9): 1–12.

Pogge, T. (2010) *Politics as Usual: What Lies behind the Pro-Poor Rhetoric*. Cambridge: Polity.

Pradella, L. (2015) 'The working poor in Western Europe: labour, poverty and global capitalism', *Comparative European Politics*, 13(5): 596–613.

Prashad, V. (2014) 'Making poverty history', *Jacobin*, www.jacobinmag. com/2014/11/making-poverty-history/.

Prashad, V. (2016) 'The class struggle is real: India is making labor history with the world's largest general strike', *Salon*, 10 September, www. salon.com/2016/09/10/the-class-struggle-is-real-india-is-making-labor-history-with-the-worlds-largest-general-strike_partner/.

Pritchett, L. (2006) 'Who is not poor? Dreaming of a world truly free of poverty', *World Bank Research Observer*, 21(1): 1–23.

Ramamurthy, P. (2004) 'Why is buying a "Madras" cotton shirt a political act? A feminist commodity chain analysis', *Feminist Studies*, 30(3): 734–69.

Ravallion, M. (2009) *Do Poorer Countries have less Capacity for Redistribution?*, Policy Research working paper no. 5046. Washington, DC: World Bank.

Ravallion, M. (2010) 'The developing world's bulging (but vulnerable) middle class', *World Development*, 38(4): 445–54.

Ravallion, M., G. Datt and D. van de Walle (1991) 'Quantifying absolute poverty in the developing world', *Review of Income and Wealth*, 37(4): 345–61.

Reardon, T., C. P. Timmer, C. B. Barrett and J. Berdegué (2003) 'The rise of supermarkets in Africa, Asia, and Latin America', *American Journal of Agricultural Economics*, 85(5): 1140–6.

Reddy, S. (2006) 'Counting the poor: the truth about world poverty statistics', *Socialist Register*, 42: 169–78.

Reddy, S., and T. Pogge (2002) *How Not to Count the Poor*. Washington, DC: World Bank.

Reddy, S., and T. Pogge (2010) 'How *not* to count the poor', in S. Anand, P. Segal and J. E. Stiglitz (eds) *Debates on the Measurement of Global Poverty*. Oxford: Oxford University Press, pp. 42–85.

Reed, A. (2014) 'Adolph Reed, Jr. responds', *New Labor Forum*, 23(1): 65–7.

Reinert, E. (ed.) (2007) *Globalization, Economic Development and Inequality: An Alternative Perspective*. Cheltenham: Edward Elgar.

Ren, H., Z. Li and E. Friedman (2016) *China on Strike: Narratives of Workers' Resistance*. Chicago: Haymarket Books.

Robinson, W. (2008) *Latin America and Global Capitalism: A Critical*

Globalization Perspective. Baltimore: Johns Hopkins University Press.

Rodrik, D. (2003) *In Search of Prosperity: Analytic Narratives on Economic Growth.* Princeton, NJ: Princeton University Press.

Rogers, D., and B. Balázs (2016) 'The view from deprivation: poverty, inequality and the distribution of wealth', in D. Cimadamore, G. Koehler and T. Pogge (eds) *Poverty and the Millennium Development Goals: A Critical Look Forward.* London: Zed Books, pp. 45–79.

Rostow, W. W. (1960) *The Stages of Economic Growth: A Non-Communist Manifesto.* Cambridge: Cambridge University Press.

Saad-Filho, A. (2010) *Growth, Poverty and Inequality: From Washington Consensus to Inclusive Growth,* UNDESA working paper no. 100. Rome: UN Department of Economic and Social Affairs.

Sachs, J. (2005) *The End of Poverty: How We Can Make it Happen in our Lifetime.* London: Penguin.

SACOM [Students & Scholars against Corporate Misbehaviour] (2010) *Workers as Machines: Military Management in Foxconn,* http://ger manwatch.org/corp/makeitfair-upd1010rep.pdf.

Said, E. (1979) *Orientalism.* New York: Vintage Books.

Schumpeter, J. A. (1987) *Capitalism, Socialism and Democracy.* London: Allen & Unwin.

Seidman, G. (1994) *Manufacturing Militance: Workers' Movements in Brazil and South Africa, 1970–1985.* Berkeley: University of California Press.

Selmeczi, A. (2012) 'Abahlali's vocal politics of proximity: speaking, suffering and political subjectivization', *Journal of Asian and African Studies,* 47(5): 498–515.

Selwyn, B. (2007) 'Labour process and workers' bargaining power in export grape production, North East Brazil', *Journal of Agrarian Change,* 7(4): 526–53.

Selwyn, B. (2008) 'Bringing social relations back in: (re)conceptualising the "Bullwhip Effect" in global commodity chains', *International Journal of Management Concepts and Philosophy,* 3(2): 156–75.

Selwyn, B. (2012) 'Beyond firm-centrism: re-integrating labour and capitalism into global commodity chain analysis', *Journal of Economic Geography,* 12(1): 205–26.

Selwyn, B. (2013) 'Social upgrading in global production networks: a critique and an alternative conception', *Competition and Change*, 17(1): 75–90.

Selwyn, B. (2014) *The Global Development Crisis*. Cambridge: Polity.

Selwyn, B. (2015a) 'Commodity chains, creative destruction and global inequality: a class analysis', *Journal of Economic Geography*, 15(2): 253–74.

Selwyn, B. (2015b) 'Friedrich Hayek: in defence of dictatorship', *Open Democracy*, 9 June, www.opendemocracy.net/benjamin-selwyn/friedrich-hayek-dictatorship.

Selwyn, B. (2015c) 'Twenty-first-century international political economy: a class-relational perspective', *European Journal of International Relations*, 21(3): 513–37.

Selwyn, B. (2016) 'Global value chains and human development: a class-relational perspective', *Third World Quarterly*, 37(10): 1768–86.

Sen, A. (1999) *Development as Freedom*. Oxford: Oxford University Press.

Sender, J. (1999) 'Africa's economic performance: limitations of the current consensus', *Journal of Economic Perspectives*, 13(3): 9–114.

Sender, J., and S. Smith (1986) *The Development of Capitalism in Africa*. London: Methuen.

Seudieu, D. (2011) 'Coffee value chain in selected importing countries', International Coffee Organization, www.ico.org/presents/1011/ICC-106-1-value-chain.pdf.

Silver, B. (2003) *Forces of Labour: Workers' Movements and Globalization since 1870*. Cambridge: Cambridge University Press.

Silver, B., and G. Arrighi (2001) 'Workers North and South', *Socialist Register*, 37: 53–76.

Silver, B., and L. Zhang (2009) 'China as an emerging epicentre of world labour unrest', in H.-F. Hung (ed.) *China and the Transformation of Global Capitalism*. Baltimore: Johns Hopkins University Press.

Sklair, L. (1993) *Assembling for Development: The Maquila Industry in Mexico and the United States*. Abingdon: Routledge.

Slaughter, M. (2009) *How U.S. Multinational Companies Strengthen the U.S. Economy*. Washington, DC: Business Roundtable and United States Council Foundation.

Smith, A. ([1776] 1976) *The Wealth of Nations.* Chicago: University of Chicago Press.

Smith, J. (2012) 'The GDP illusion: value added versus value capture', *Monthly Review* 64(3), http://monthlyreview.org/2012/07/01/the-gdp-illusion/.

Smith, J. (2016) *Imperialism in the Twenty-First Century: Globalization, Super-Exploitation, and Capitalism's Final Crisis.* New York: Monthly Review Press.

Solow, R. (1988) 'What is labour-market flexibility? What is it good for?', Keynes Lecture, *Proceedings of the British Academy,* 97: 189–211.

Souza, M. (2007) 'Social movements as "critical urban planning" agents', *City: Analysis of Urban Trends, Culture, Policy, Action,* 10(3): 327–42.

Standing, G. (1989) 'Global feminization through flexible labour', *World Development,* 17(7): 1077–95.

Starrs, S. (2014) 'The chimera of global governance', *New Left Review,* 87(May–June): 81–96.

Steans, J., and D. Tepe (2010) 'Introduction – Social reproduction in international political economy: theoretical insights and inter-national, transnational and local sitings', *Review of International Political Economy,* 17(5): 807–15.

Stédile, J. P. (2004) 'El MST y las disputas por las alternativas en Brasil', *Osal,* 5(13): 31–9; http://biblioteca.clacso.edu.ar//ar/libros/osal/osal13/ACStedile.pdf.

Stiglitz, J. E. (1998) 'More instruments and broader goals: moving toward the post-Washington consensus', WIDER Annual Lecture 2. Helsinki: World Institute for Development Economics Research (UNU/WIDER); http://citeseerx.ist.psu.edu/viewdoc/download?doi=10.1.1.201.2709&rep=rep1&type=pdf.

Stiglitz, J. E. (2007) *Making Globalization Work.* New York: W. W. Norton.

Strange, R., and J. Newton (2006) 'Stephen Hymer and the externaliza-tion of production', *International Business Review,* 15(2): 180–93.

Sumner, A. (2016) *Global Poverty: Deprivation, Distribution and Development.* Oxford: Oxford University Press.

Swinnen, J. F. M., and A. Vandeplas (2010) 'Market power and rents in global supply chains', *Agricultural Economics,* 41: 109–20.

Taglioni, D., and D. Winkler (2014) *Making Global Value Chains Work for Development*. Washington, DC: World Bank.

Thompson, E. P. (1963) *The Making of the English Working Class*. New York: Pantheon.

Thompson, N. (2012) 'Does Apple have a bruise?' *New Yorker* (4 October).

Trainer, T. (1996) *Towards a Sustainable Economy*. Oxford: Jon Carpenter.

Tugal, C. (2016) *The Fall of the Turkish Model: How the Arab Uprisings Brought Down Islamic Liberalism*. London: Verso.

UNCTAD [United Nations Conference on Trade and Development] (2003) *World Investment Report 2003: FDI Policies for Development: National and International Perspectives*. New York and Geneva: United Nations.

UNCTAD [United Nations Conference on Trade and Development] (2013) *Global Value Chains and Development: Investment and Value Added Trade in the Global Economy*. New York: United Nations.

UNIDO [United Nations Industrial Development Organization] (2006) *Yearbook of Industrial Statistics*. New York: United Nations.

UNIDO [United Nations Industrial Development Organization] (2011) *Industrial Development Report*. New York: United Nations.

Upchurch, M. (2014) 'The internet, social media and the workplace', *International Socialism*, no. 141, http://isj.org.uk/the-internet-social-media-and-the-workplace/.

Varoufakis, Y. (2011) *The Global Minotaur*. Chicago: University of Chicago Press.

Vergara-Camus, L. (2014) *Land and Freedom: The MST, the Zapatistas and Peasant Alternatives to Neoliberalism*. London: Zed Books.

Vogel, L. (2013) *Marxism and the Oppression of Women: Toward a Unitary Theory*. Leiden: Brill.

Wade, R. (1990) *Governing the Market: Economic Theory and the Role of Government in East Asian Industrialization*. Princeton, NJ: Princeton University Press.

Wade, R. (2004) 'Is globalization reducing poverty and inequality?', *World Development*, 32(4): 567–89.

Wade, R. (2008) 'Globalization, growth, poverty, inequality, resentment, and imperialism', in J. Ravenhill (ed.) *Global Political Economy*. 2nd edn, Oxford: Oxford University Press, pp. 373–409.

Walker, R., and D. Buck (2007) 'The Chinese road', *New Left Review*, 46(July–August), https://newleftreview.org/II/46/richard-walker-daniel-buck-the-chinese-road.

Warren, B. (1980) *Imperialism: Pioneer of Capitalism*. London: New Left Books.

Weber, M. (1978) *Economy and Society*. Berkeley: University of California Press.

Weeks, K. (2011) *The Problem with Work: Feminism, Marxism, Antiwork Politics, and Postwork Imaginaries*. Durham, NC, and London: Duke University Press.

Weis, A. J. (2007) *The Global Food Economy: The Battle for the Future of Farming*. London: Zed Books.

Weis, T. (2010) 'The accelerating biophysical contradictions of industrial capitalist agriculture', *Journal of Agrarian Change*, 10(3): 315–41.

Welch, C. (2006) 'Globalization and the transformation of work in rural Brazil: agribusiness, rural labour unions and peasant mobilization', *International Labour and Working Class History*, 70(1): 35–60.

Werner, M., J. Bair and V. Fernández (2014) 'Linking up to development? Global value chains and the making of a post-Washington Consensus', *Development and Change*, 45(6): 1219–47.

Whalen, C. (2005) 'Sending jobs offshore from the United States', *Intervention: A Journal of Economics*, 2(2): 33–40.

Wilson, K. (1999) 'Patterns of accumulation and struggles of rural labour: some aspects of agrarian change in central Bihar', *Journal of Peasant Studies*, 26(2–3): 316–54.

Wilson, K. (2008) 'Reclaiming "agency", reasserting resistance', *IDS Bulletin*, 39(6): 83–91.

Winant, H. (2004) *The New Politics of Race: Globalism, Difference, Justice*. Minneapolis: University of Minnesota Press.

Wolf, M. (2005) *Why Globalization Works*. 2nd edn, New Haven, CT: Yale University Press.

Wolford, W. (2005) 'Agrarian moral economies and neoliberalism in Brazil: competing worldviews and the state in the struggle for land', *Environment and Planning A*, 37(2): 241–61.

Wolford, W. (2010) *This Land is Ours Now: Social Mobilization and the Meanings of Land in Brazil.* Durham, NC: Duke University Press.

Wood, E. (1981) 'The separation of the economic and political in capitalism', *New Left Review*, 127(May–June): 66.

Wood, E. M. (2012) *Liberty and Property: A Social History of Western Political Thought from Renaissance to Enlightenment.* London: Verso.

Woodward, D. (2010) *How Poor is Poor?* London: New Economics Foundation.

Woodward, D. (2015) '*Incrementum ad absurdum*: global growth, inequality and poverty eradication in a carbon-constrained world', *World Economic Review*, 4: 43–62.

World Bank (1990) *World Development Report 1990: Poverty.* New York: Oxford University Press.

World Bank (1993) *The East Asian Miracle.* Oxford: Oxford University Press.

Yeates, N. (2004) 'Global care chains', *International Feminist Journal of Politics*, 6(3): 369–91.

Zeilig, L. (2010) 'Tony Cliff: deflected permanent revolution in Africa', *International Socialism*, no. 126: 159–186; www.isj.org.uk/?id=641

Zikode, S. (2013) 'Despite the state's violence, our fight to escape the mud and fire of South Africa's slums will continue', *The Guardian*, 11 November, www.theguardian.com/commentisfree/2013/nov/11/south-africa-fight-decent-housing-assassination.

Zobel, G. (2009) 'We are millions', *New Internationalist*, no. 428, https://newint.org/features/special/2009/12/01/we-are-millions/.

Zorzoli, L. (2016) 'Not one less', *Jacobin*, www.jacobinmag.com/2016/11/argentina-femicide-strike-women-unions-sexism/.

Index

purchasing power parity (PPP)
World Bank and 23–4, 26–7

race and ethnicity
capitalist social forces and 43
democratic development and
150
discrimination 127
imperialism and 43–4
indigenous peoples and 145–6
oppression and 14
Ravallion, Martin
poverty measurement and 23
rising middle class 31–4
Reclaiming Development (Chang and
Grabel) 8
Reddy, Sanjay
poverty lines and 4–5
World Bank poverty analysis 24–5
redistribution of wealth
democratic development and
134–7
Reinert, Erik 7
Ricardo, David
comparative advantage 81–2
statist political economy 92
Rodrik, Dani 7
Rogers, Deborah 136
Romania
minimum/living wage 62
Rostow, W. E.
modernisation theory 78–9
The Stages of Economic Growth 78
Russia
counter-revolution 129
labour-driven development 11
Stalinism and 95–6
workers' revolution 128–9

Sachs, Jeffrey 34
Schumpeter, Joseph 50
Sen, Amartya 7
Sender, John 97–8
sexuality, oppression and 14
shack dwellers' movements 107–10
Shenton, Roger 77–8, 79–80
slavery and serfdom
pre-capitalist 36

Slovakia
minimum/living wage 62
Smith, Adam 81, 159n4
Smith, Sheila 97
social care
universal basic income and 140–1
social justice
capitalist doublethink and 4
social neoliberalism 86–7
social relations
capital and labour 106–7
capitalist social factory 40
class and 14–15
racism 43–5
reproduction costs 57
social reproduction theory 13
socialism
state capitalism 96, 129
society
absorption of the state by 130–4
communal need/purposes 131–4
solidarity
racism and 44
Solow, Robert 83–4
South Africa
1995 Freedom Charter 141
anti-eviction movement 109
mine/metalworkers 108, 110–11
platinum mine workers 42
shack dwellers' movements
107–10
student struggles 19
worker revolts 19
South Korea
Apple and 69
protests against Park Guen-hye 19
statist political economy 93–5
Sri Lanka
minimum/living wage 62
The Stages of Economic Growth
(Rostow) 78
Stalin, Joseph 95–6, 128
Starrs, Sean 54
state leaders
doublethink 1–2
states
capital–labour relations and 106–7
decent work concept 90–1